STAY LOW, MOVE FAST, TRUST NO ONE

By Mike Jones-Mathias

THE BEGINNING

It was the eighth of May 2003, and I took a call on my mobile phone while sitting in my office.

'Fancy setting up a security company?' asked Steve.

'Yeah, sure. We've talked about it enough, so let's do it,' I replied.

Steve Brierley was an old Army mate of mine and now worked as a business development manager for a local manned guarding company in South Wales called Scorpion. I, on the other hand, had traded one uniform for another and had joined the "boys in blue". I had completed just over six years and was now a detective sergeant based at Risca in the Gwent Police. Steve and I had often talked about setting up our own security company, with me running the operational side and Steve bringing in the business, at which he had proven to be good. Since leaving the Army only two years prior he had nearly doubled the turnover of Scorpion.

'In Iraq' was the brief but succinct response from Steve.

Thinking he was joking, I replied, 'Well, we'll need to complete a recce, so you'd better book some tickets.'

'OK. Leave it with me' said Steve and hung up.

Not really giving it too much thought, I returned to the crime detection rates within the sector area for which I was responsible. After all, I was in the enviable position of doing a job where I actually looked forward to going to work. Modesty aside, I was good at it, and I got a lot of job satisfaction. Not to mention that it was a decent wage with the overtime: I was making over forty grand a year and had more than overtaken my last wage on leaving the Army some six years earlier.

Four days later, Steve called again. 'I've booked some

tickets for next week, so you'd better sort some leave out.'

'No problem,' I replied, still thinking this was some sort of joke.

'Come around after work, and we can talk this through,' said Steve.

'You serious?' I asked with a little excitement.

'Why not? I've been speaking to SO, and he suggested we have a look at it,' said Steve.

SO was Col. Stephen Owen Thomas, the current British defence attaché in Kuwait. Steve had known him for many years, and I had met him a few times socially. SO had been out in the Middle East for several years and was well connected with what was happening in regards to the whole Iraq business. After the Invasion (or Liberation, depending on your point of view) of Iraq, SO had suggested that Iraq was now a lawless and hostile country and any company wanting to work there would need private ex-pat security. It would be a gold rush. He had been approached by other security companies for assistance to open doors, as he was in quite an influential position. He was getting close to retirement and, as a serving Army officer, could not be seen to be connected commercially with any civilian set-up.

I pulled up at Steve's house in Rudry, a very nice old farmhouse set on about two acres of ground. Detached from the main house was a rather large shed affair that contained a small gym, an office, and a bar. He had moved to the farmhouse a year or so earlier after marrying his third wife, Diane. She was a well-paid accountant, and together they had a baby daughter.

Upon arriving, I also noticed Ian's clapped-out old Cavalier parked up. Ian Russell was an Aussie and had been in the UK for some years. He had divorced a year or two earlier and was busy trying to get himself back on this feet after his wife had taken him to the cleaners. He was an ex-Australian Army and, apart from renovating property, was also a captain with 21 SAS, the Territorial Army, and often disappeared for a week or so at a time.

I had known Ian for a few years and had assisted him in trying to set up his own company, again within the security industry. He was trying to secure a contract providing guys in the oil industry in Algeria. He was working in Algeria as a security guard himself, so he could not be seen to be chasing the contract; he had approached me to act as the front man. We had dabbled around for several months, but nothing had come of it as Ian always wanted to cross all the t's and dot all the i's. One thing I had come to learn was that sometimes you have just got to grasp the nettle and go for it. I'd had very little experience at business, but even I could see that he would get nowhere without taking a few risks. For my efforts, which were considerable, I would get 25 per cent of the profits if anything resulted from it all.

I joined Steve and Ian at the bar.

'So we're going to stroll into probably the most hostile country in the world and ask anyone if they want to hire us?' I asked.

'Pretty much so,' said Steve. 'SO reckons that there is huge potential for private armed security in Iraq post-liberation. There will be billions thrown at this, and we can have a slice of the pie.'

'OK, this is a serious suggestion then? We will need to get out there and suss out the situation and see what's what. From there we can decide if this is a goer,' I said.

We proceeded to theorise on how we would do this. Steve would deal with business development and chase potential clients. He had the gift of the gab and was very good at getting in front of people. My concern was that Steve was a rather large guy. He was six foot four and must have weighed around twenty-four stone. He did not exactly look the part of a highly tuned security operative. But he was a larger-than-life character, and I did have confidence in his ability to get our foot in the door commercially. I had my doubts that he would be able to effectively organise a security operation. He had completed a tour in Northern Ireland but had spent most of the tour either in the control room or playing rugby, as in his earlier life he had been an accomplished second row. Civvie Street had piled on the pounds . . . and then some.

Ian would act as team leader on the ground. After all, he was in the SAS, albeit the Territorial Army, and would be far better than any of us at close-quarter tactics. I also did not want him too close to the business side of things, as he would potentially slow the whole decision-making process down.

My role was to look after the operational management. I had attended the Royal Military Academy Sandhurst and had been commissioned as an officer into the Corps of Royal Engineers at the age of nineteen. I had spent twelve years in the Army and a further five years in the Territorial Army. I had completed tours of duties as Combat Engineer, Bomb Disposal, and Specialist Counter Terrorist Search. I had deployed on the first Gulf War, Operation Granby as the Brits called it or Operation Desert Storm as our cousins across the pond called it. I had risen to the rank of Major. Consequently, I believed I would be best experienced at looking after the operational side of things. I also liked the idea that I would be sitting in the ops room, coordinating operations rather than being out on the ground, where a lot of people wanted to shoot or blow up a Westerner. It was all looking pretty good, from what I could see.

'So you booked tickets?' I asked Steve.

'No, not yet,' Steve replied. 'SO suggests we wait until he can organise some meetings for us. We can go over to Kuwait for a week and get in as many meetings as possible.'

Over dinner that night I broached the subject with Carole, my wife. She was concerned over the danger aspect but I reassured her that I would be based in the ops room in Kuwait. We discussed the fact that I would effectively be throwing away a career in the police with all the implications of that. I explained that I would not hand in my resignation until I was pretty certain that this crazy idea was going to work! She had never really liked Steve, and we had many discussions over whether I could trust him. Steve had always blagged his way and sailed close to the wind. I explained that I fully expected him to milk expenses and suspected he would always be tempted to fiddle a fast buck if he could. But I knew I could trust him to watch my back, and I was certain he would never double-cross me. We had been mates for fifteen years. After much discussion on trust Carole and I decided it was worth going ahead.

RECCE TO KUWAIT

A few weeks went by, and I was getting a little impatient. I was more than happy in my job, but in the back of my mind, there was this niggling feeling reminding me of the potential of something more exciting. SO still had not come back to us with any confirmed meetings or plans, and I was starting to have my doubts as to whether anything was going to happen at all. Then on 1 July 2003, two months after our initial informal planning session, SO announced there was to be a 'business in Iraq' forum held in the British embassy in Kuwait the following week. I was currently working on a murder case and was right in the thick of it, feeling very sad for the victim and their family, but appreciating that as a detective this was what it was all about. We do not get many murder cases, and apart from being interesting they are also great for overtime. I approached my detective inspector and requested leave, stating personal reasons. Thankfully, he did not ask too many questions and granted me leave for a week. At last we could get going on something and I booked flight tickets immediately.

Steve, Ian, and I met again and discussed how we were to present ourselves. Ian wanted to go under the guise of the company he had tried to set up, COMSEC. It was registered in Jersey, and we would all be equal partners. As an alternative, Steve had been approached by Securiforce, a local man-guarding company in South Wales, to go on board as their business development director. They had offered him the opportunity to buy into the company. Steve suggested we use this link as a credible backdrop to what we were to do in the Middle East. Securiforce had various accreditations, and we assessed this would come in handy if due diligence was to be carried out. Ian was not totally convinced, but we all eventually agreed we would go with Securiforce. We had some business cards and a load of company brochures made up, and therewith, Securiforce International was born — or at least the concept was.

Steve told Ian and me that the two other partners in Securiforce did not want to be involved with the international operations side as neither of them were ex-military and they did not want any potential litigations resulting from almost certain acts of violence that would occur. This suited us just fine as more partners meant less profit share.

On the seventh of July 2003 British Airways flew Steve, Ian, and me to Kuwait. It was an overnight flight, and we arrived tired but full of excitement. At this time one needed a visa arranged before you could travel in Kuwait. Upon landing, we were met straight off the aircraft by SO, complete in his full uniform with lots of braid and tassels. With his diplomatic status, he was permitted to come right into the secure-arrivals section of the airport and personally hand us our visas.

We cleared through immigration and collected our bags. We walked out of the airport building, and BANG, it hit us. The heat was intense. We expected it to be hot, but Jesus Christ, this was something else. There was almost a background noise to the heat. Strange, I know, but that was my first impression; one could actually hear the heat.

SO provided us with the ambassador's armoured Mercedes 4×4 to get to the hotel. While not really needed in Kuwait, this was more likely SO showing off. We booked in at the Crowne Plaza Hotel and had a quick brief from SO. He had arranged a meeting for Steve and Ian with a potential sponsor while I was to go to the embassy for the business forum. So off I went for a quick shower before getting suited, booted, and ready for the first official action of Securiforce International.

SO and I arrived at the embassy by 0900 hrs and proceeded to go through security. He explained to me that he had ensured there were to be no other security company representative at the forum. Others had approached him, but he had declined their requests to attend. Most attendees present were construction, engineering, and transportation companies all wanting to gain a better understanding of what was required to be able to operate in Iraq. All present were British companies, of course, and all were wanting a bit of the potential lucrative market that was to open up.

The forum kicked off with a couple of presentations from various speakers outlining the affiliations that were being forged with various Iraqi companies and what the audience needed to do to become part of the whole affair. Quite frankly, it was evident that most of the speakers had not been inside of Iraq and were unable to answer many of the questions put to them from the floor. Then SO gave a presentation about the threat and security situation. He made much of the fact that most information had been provided by MI6 and that it was confidential and not to be discussed outside of the forum. Perhaps a little dramatic, but it did have the desired effect of stirring up a male audience with fantasies of being James Bond. He gave a brief history of Iraq and outlined the current level of violence. There were many shootings, mostly of a criminal nature, which were centred more around Baghdad and within the 'Sunni Triangle' (Baghdad, Tikrit, and Ramadi). He stressed that under no circumstances should anyone consider going into Iraq without private security protection.

Following the presentations and question time, we all mingled over coffee and dates. Quite suddenly I found myself the centre of attention. A buzz had spread around the forum that I was a representative of a private security company. It seemed everyone wanted to meet me. One thing that Sandhurst taught me was to stand on my hind legs and talk absolute bollocks with confidence. I handed out business cards like confetti and blagged my way trying to convince those who asked that we were an established company and had men and equipment ready and available to deploy. As a result of the forum I came away with three firm meetings and another two to be confirmed. By the end of the day we were to have meetings planned all week.

After the forum, SO invited me to the embassy bar for a bite to eat, which constituted a plate of sandwiches washed down with a few cans of Stella. I had been in the country for less than six hours, and I was at a bar, drinking an ice-cold lager—not bad for a state that bans alcohol.

On my return to the hotel, I met up with Steve and Ian. Their meeting had been less fruitful. It turned out the men they had met were a couple of ex–British Military guys who were working for Securicor and wanted to do some sort of joint venture guarding a contractor's compound somewhere in Iraq. Securicor was a multinational security company and one of the big players already in Iraq. It all sounded a bit dodgy to me, and my impression was that they were just trying to glean information from us—rather amusing, as in reality we were none the wiser. Throughout the week we had several meetings, all of which appeared to be leading nowhere. The most likely prospect was a visit to a chemical plant that produced chlorine and was transporting it to a plant in Basra. I tried to explain the consequences of the bad guys getting ahold of a large cylinder of chlorine and having it explode at the gate of a military base. With the wind in the right direction, it would be lethal over a wide area.

On the ninth of July we again made use of the ambassador's armoured 4×4. However, this time we also 'borrowed' four 9 millimetre Browning pistols and an AK-47 from the embassy armoury, courtesy of SO. We made our way up Route 80 towards the Kuwait/Iraq border. About five hundred metres short of the border, we stopped and donned our body armour from the rear of the vehicle. We loaded a magazine into our pistols and headed for the border crossing point. When we reached the border, the US Military were controlling access. There was a simple barrier across the road, and on seeing the diplomatic plates on our vehicle, the soldier raised the barrier and threw up a salute as we carried on past. We were now in Iraq.

Immediately the deprivation was apparent. As we made our way through the small border village of Safwan, it was like something out of the Dark Ages. There were lots of small, low-level huts, many showing signs of warfare, with bullet holes scattered all over them. This would have been the first place the Liberating Forces would have come through. My eyes were everywhere. Although in a B6 armoured vehicle capable of protecting us against small-arms fire, I was conscious that we had no backup, and even run-flat tyres have their limitations. We made only a short fifteen-minute drive to Umm Qasr Port, where a small UK Military base was set up. Umm Qasr Port was the only sea-access point in Iraq. As we approached, I could see many adult Iraqi males, each with an AK-47. We quickly assessed they were some form of security for the port. We drove slowly through this outer cordon and into the inner camp, where the UK Military security was a lot tighter. However, again on seeing the diplomatic plates, we were shown straight in. SO disappeared into the headquarters building, and the three of us waited by the vehicle.

After waiting about ten minutes, SO returned, and we drove across the compound to meet with Ian Lang, a South African. He was the representative of Inchcape and was responsible for the security of the port area. Inchcape operates worldwide as freight forwarders and specialise mostly at ports and also handle much of the logistics for the Royal Navy. We had been told that as the port was opening up more for business, the provision of security needed to be better in order to attract commercial companies and give them confidence. However, on driving around the port area, it was apparent that the so-called security was no more than the local guys we'd witnessed carrying AK-47s. As we drove along the quayside we approached what looked like a small cordon of armed men around a truck loading tyres from a ship. I asked Ian if they were the security. He explained that they were local criminals and they were stealing the tyres. As I looked more closely I could see that the ship's crew were being held at gunpoint on the deck as the bad guys helped themselves to the cargo. Ian calmly explained that as long as we were not interested in them, they would not be interested in us. Plus, our pistols would be no match against their assault rifles. We continued our tour of the port perimeter, where I could see large sections of the fence missing. Ian further explained that the bad guys would threaten the local security guys, telling them that they knew where they lived and to turn a blind eye to any and all criminal activity. Then they would drive in with a fleet of truck and steal whatever they wanted. Three nights earlier a convoy of trucks had come in and stolen several thousand bags of milk powder stored in the World Food Program warehouse. I could see why the security needed attention.

As we made our way back to the border, we stopped briefly at a large bomb-damaged building. In one of the forum meetings, we'd discussed providing security to a hotel that had suffered a lot of bomb damage and was soon to be restored. We got out from the safety of the armoured vehicle, and very soon thereafter a couple of local kids appeared from nowhere. There were two little girls no older than five or six, dressed in rags and looking up at us with their big brown eyes. It was not us they were interested in but the bottles of water we were each carrying in our hands. Steve opened the back of the wagon and gave them a couple of bottles each; within seconds we were surrounded by kids of all ages. My eyes were again everywhere, looking into the distance for any other movement from the small buildings about fifty metres away. The good feeling of seeing the delight on these kids' faces quickly vanished, and I suddenly felt uncomfortable. I saw a small group of adult males huddled around the side of a hut and could see at least two AK-47s. I immediately removed my pistol from its holster. I guess kids in the UK would have scattered in all directions on seeing a weapon produced — these kids did not even bat an eyelid. I suggested we get back on the wagon and head off.

As we neared the border heading back into Kuwait, the soldier again obliged as we drove through. A few hundred metres down the road we pulled over to remove our body armour and unload the pistols. Later, Steve told me that Ian appeared not to know how to unload the Browning pistol. This was a little worrying, as it was standard issue and he should have been able to do this blindfolded.

On our last evening in Kuwait we had a meeting with a Kiwi who wanted to bring in a small ship into the port of Umm Qasr to act as a floating hotel for contractors. He was interested in armed security. Ian and he got on well, and after the rather large meal we were leaving, I noticed Ian handing this Kiwi chap his COMSEC business card. I shot a glance at Steve and could see he had also caught this. Back at the hotel we confronted Ian; he explained that he just wanted to give the Kiwi some personal contact details. Ian became very defensive, and I began seriously having doubts about his loyalty.

From the week in Kuwait, we realised that the big boys in security services were already in the country and well established. It had been four months since the Liberation, and many of the more established companies, like CRG, ArmorGroup, Olive, and Stirling, had already arrived on the coat-tails of their global clients. However, what was apparent was that all of them were concentrating on close protection and static guards. Many referred to this as bodyguarding, but I believe this to be more specific to where an individual is going to be targeted. In Iraq it was more an opportunist attack that one was trying to counter, and I believe close protection was a better description. The static guarding consisted more of either guarding accommodation compounds or installations such as power plants. However, from the forum I'd learned that an expected 70 per cent of the material to rebuild Iraq's infrastructure would enter via Kuwait. Nearly all of that would need to be transported by roads, and from what we had discovered, there was nobody providing this service — at least not outside of the military. At this stage all convoys of trucks going upcountry were escorted by military. At some point the military would stop doing this, and there would be a huge market for convoy protection. We decided this is where our future lay and would set up accordingly.

We returned to the UK, and I back to work as a detective sergeant. I quickly got back into the swing of things and began to wonder if I really wanted to give up all of this for what was, at best, some uncertainty and, at the worst, very dangerous. I knew I would have to go into Iraq at some point, but in the main I would be based in Kuwait.

We agreed that the next step was to find a Kuwaiti sponsor. If we were set up in Kuwait to escort convoys into Iraq, we would need a local. We all stumped up five thousand pounds to fund Steve to head back to Kuwait to look for a sponsor with SO's help. I was a little concerned, as Steve was not the most careful when it came to money, especially when he was spending someone else's. He had become the consummate professional when it came to expense accounts, but I was learning that you needed to appear as a major player to be taken seriously. So it was five-star hotels and lots of rubbing shoulders with potential decision-makers. Within a few weeks, Steve headed back to Kuwait to begin the hunt for a sponsor and potential clients.

RECRUITING

I began the process of recruiting for our security guards. We were going to need guys and, quite possibly, at short notice. Until Iraq, the private-security business — or the Circuit, as it was known — was very much a Special Forces closed shop. But with the sudden explosion in sheer security personnel numbers needed, any guy who had ever picked up a weapon came forward. I needed to set some criteria. I decided that as a minimum, any candidate had to have at least five years of military experience, completed at least one operational tour, and must not have been out of the military for more than the time he had served. I posted an advert with the Regular Forces Employment Agency (RFEA), an outfit funded by the government to help ex-forces find civvie employment. I was quickly inundated with CVs from every branch of the military. Surprisingly, many did not meet the criteria I had set, and so many were paper sifted. I split the candidates down by geographical region and decided to hold interviews in Cardiff, Reading, and Leeds. I drew up a list of questions I wanted to follow to establish what sort of guy I was interviewing. I did not want a knuckle-dragging grunt (infantryman) who would be fine handling a weapon but would become an administrative burden due to his lack of initiative and inability to look after his personal affairs. A lot of ex-forces find it difficult to settle back into Civvie Street because they are used to the military looking after their personal affairs, such as pay, meals, etc. I was looking for guys who could bring more than just their military skills. I wanted guys who would be able to understand the requirements and politics of clients, appreciating that there is a commercial aspect to what we would be doing. I devised a series of scenarios and asked candidates what their decision-making process would be in certain circumstances with lots of 'what if's'. From our short recce, I had a slight feel for what it was going to be like, but mostly my process was based on assumptions and theories—perhaps not a good starting point, but that was all I had.

I was also advised by a friend of a friend who was former SAS that I should avoid taking anyone from the SAS. He explained that they would always feel superior in their ability to run things and would eventually try and steal your contracts from under you. And, as they were former SAS, the clients would likely be inclined to go with them. The Special Air Service had a reputation as one of the best elite special forces of any nation. Their selection and training was extremely tough, but their results spoke for themselves. The Iranian embassy siege in London in 1980 had brought them to the world's attention with the successful rescue of all hostages without loss of life, with the exception of the terrorist with all but one killed.

Throughout July and August I interviewed about fifty guys. Some gave me the answers I saw as correct, while others were way off the mark. One scenario I used described a convoy approaching a small village in the middle of nowhere and up ahead a local male was waving down the lead vehicle. In this scenario, I was looking for a candidate who would consider stopping the convoy short and getting all guards out on the ground to provide all-round defence. Thereafter the candidate would have the local male approach under the cover of our armed guys. I also wanted the candidate to consider all the possibilities of an ambush, snipers, roadside bombs, etc. The better candidates would give this response, whereas the weaker ones talked about running the male over and carrying on. Not really what I wanted!

I then explained that the male was simply asking for water, so 'What do you do?' The better candidates would state they would be firm but friendly and would not give water. The rationale being that if water was given, then the next time there would be more wanting water, and the next time even more. This had been shown on our short recce into Iraq, where Steve had given the little girl a bottle and we were soon surrounded. The weaker candidates would give water and, when asked about the implications of the increasing number of future requests, suggested that the convoy took a water tanker. This was an option, but our job was to provide security for our clients' trucks, and we could not be sidetracked by trying to sort out the humanitarian problems of Iraq. While perhaps this approach was a little alien to soldiers who have been taught to win the 'hearts and minds', this was not the military, and we were not there for this sort of work.

The scenario would continue with a warning from the male that a large group of about twenty men had arrived in their village earlier in the day and were heavily armed, so 'What do you do?' The weaker candidates would say to turn the convoy around and go back. Others would say to carry on and, if ambushed, to fight through. On a commercial basis, turning around every time there was a potential threat was not acceptable, but neither was blindly driving into a potential ambush. The better candidates would consider sending a recce forward to assess the danger. I was looking for them to come out with all the combat indicators, such as lookouts, deserted streets, and blockages in the road to slow or stop a convoy, but also working on the old adage that if it looks like an ambush, then it probably is.

I would continue the scenario then, saying that all indicators were present that there was a heavily armed ambush waiting for the convoy, so 'What do you do?' One candidate, an ex–Royal Marine staff sergeant, wanted to wait until nightfall and then send in a team to creep up and take out the bad guys. This was possibly a solution if clearing the route was a key military objective in a war setting. However, the intention was to provide security, earn some money, and all come out alive. The preferred option was to inform the coalition forces, as the military would be interested in such a group of insurgents and they would be best equipped to deal with it.

I had a whole mix of guys coming forward. I began to learn what various regiments had been doing over the past twenty years. Being based in Cardiff, I ended up interviewing many from the Welsh regiments: Royal Regiment of Wales, Welsh Guards, Royal Welsh, and of course, the Paras (paratroopers), who were coming out of the woodwork from everywhere. I also had candidates from some of the Royal Corps, such as engineers, signals, and transport. I'd been advised by others that only infantry should be selected, but I believed that the British Army was generally successful because of the various mix of regiments and corps, each with its own set of unique skills to offer. Some argued that drivers from transport regiments would be no use as they were not skilled enough in infantry tactics. But again, I believed that on operational tours it was these very drivers who had been doing convoy drills and, if anything, were better placed to understand the problems associated with moving a convoy of up to twenty trucks. Plus I needed to consider that we may have a need for bomb disposal and/or search skills from the engineers.

As a result of the interviews I began to build a database of those I deemed successful candidates. Some were the old and bold, such as Dominic Grey. He was a full-career ex-para and a Falklands veteran, infamous within the para reg for being shot in the head during the Falklands and having undergone surgery while still awake. He was also a hell of a character, to boot. There was also Andy Christie (Chalky), an ex-sergeant from the Devon and Dorset Regiment. He was a straight-up-and-down NCO (noncommissioned officer) and, on first meeting, I thought, would be a good asset bringing his own sense of discipline to the team. Then there was Ray Clark, an ex-marine and current serving firearms officer with the South Wales Police. He was very civilianised but had a quiet, strong common sense about him. On the other end of the spectrum was Richard Stanly (Stan). Although he was a young lad, he had served six years and had been a member of the Royal Artillery's Special OP (Observation Post). This unit was basically a bunch of guys who would operate behind enemy lines, calling in artillery and air strikes—not quite the SAS, but their selection was reputedly as tough. My first reaction was that he was too young and too immature, but upon further reflection, I believed that he added a good mix to some of the old dogs.

The truth of the matter was that none of us really knew what to plan for, as the whole Iraq scenario was new. It was too soon after the Liberation for the availability of Iraq vets. I was basing my assumptions on my own experience of the First Gulf War and from our very brief recce. But the one thing I knew for sure was that the Army system, whatever its shortcomings, was a system that worked, and those I recruited would have the basics ingrained into them. I wanted to set up the company along military lines because I knew it worked. But I also wanted to recruit guys based on merit judged by the criteria I had devised. I was not overly keen on 'mates of'; I have always been wary of guys bringing in their mates, as was often the case, who then never really stepped up to the mark.

As the recruiting went on, I had to be careful as I was also still a serving police officer. There are a lot of links with ex-military and police, and the last thing I needed was to be compromised. I would have landed in hot water had it been revealed I was busy recruiting for a private security venture, especially if the whole thing never even got off the ground.

By early September, Steve was no further forward on sponsor, and there was definitely no sniff of a potential contract.

THE IAN SPLIT

Mid-September, Steve returned to the UK still empty-handed. He called me and asked me to go around to see him. Over a coffee he told me how he had received a phone call from the Kiwi we had met in Kuwait who wanted to bring the floating hotel into Umm Qasr Port. He had called Steve from Heathrow, asking if Steve knew where Ian was, as Ian was late for their meeting. Not knowing what meeting he was referring to, Steve played along and probed a little further and established that Ian had been negotiating a security contract with the Kiwi outside of Securiforce. We had a conference call with SO, who was still in Kuwait. The consensus was that Ian was not really bringing anything to the party and, as SO so eloquently put it, 'He's a little shit, and I never really liked or trusted him'. Steve and I decided we would get Ian around and challenge him, and based on his response, we would make a decision on what direction we would take.

The following day, I was at work, and Steve called to say Ian was going to go to Steve's house for midday. I agreed to nip out from work and meet up. Just before twelve I arrived at Steve's. Ian was yet to get there. Steve then expressed his opinion that Ian should go. I tended to agree, and we decided that whatever the discussion, we would both remain on the course that Ian was to leave the partnership. Ian soon arrived, and we began. At first Ian appeared to be relaxed. Then Steve asked him what his intentions were in meeting the Kiwi. Ian's mood changed, and I could feel the tension mounting. Ian explained that he had been speaking with the Kiwi regarding some guards to escort him into Iraq.

'So what about men, vehicles, weapons, passes, etc.?' I

asked. 'You would need all that planned.'

'Yeah, of course,' replied Ian.

'So when were you going to mention this to us?' I probed.

I could see Ian's face, and I had interviewed enough suspects to know when someone's mind was racing to think of what to say.

'Well I ...' And he paused long enough for me to become even more suspicious. 'I was going to tell you when it was more certain,' Ian said. I was then waiting for Steve to step in and challenge Ian over the fact that the Kiwi had told him that they were discussing the contract outside of Securiforce. Steve sat silent, just looking at the floor. I wasn't sure if he was thinking or was so angry he couldn't look at Ian or was simply trying to avoid being involved in the conversation.

With nothing coming from Steve and after about thirty seconds of silence, I eventually said, 'I understand that you were discussing doing this under COMSEC.' This was a bluff on my behalf, but an educated guess that it was accurate. I could see that Ian's breathing was deepening and his mouth was dry. He swallowed hard and replied, 'I was only using COMSEC because it is already a registered company and I ... well, thought it would be better, and we could always change it over to Securiforce later.'

'But we had discussed this at length that we would use Securiforce,' I snapped back. Steve remained motionless and silent. I was looking for some backup. Ian began waffling about company registration and due diligence. Meanwhile, my mind was racing. I thought about Ian and his value to the whole venture. Disregarding the current issue of going outside the partnership, I could not actually see what he was going to bring to the party. I guessed he would be OK as a shooter out on the ground, but as far as setting up and running the company, I could only see him as a hindrance. I quickly decided that I would stick to the plan that he was to leave. Ian was still in full flow when I interrupted him and said, 'The thing is, Jas, is that we have all got to trust each other if we are to go into business together. And I am not so sure that I can trust you after this.'

Steve continued to be a statue.

'You talk about trust. You told me you don't trust Steve,' said Ian.

Ian had previously asked me whether I trusted Steve. I had explained that I expected Steve to blag some expenses and that I could live with that. But I had stated that I trusted him to go into business with him.

I realised that Ian was going for the counter-attack and try and set Steve and me against each other. From Steve's silence I doubted for a second and wondered if Steve was waiting to see who came out of this the stronger. After all, it was Steve who held the ace card in that he was the one who was closest to SO and without him this whole thing was not going to work. I tried to defuse Ian's counter by looking him straight in the eye and saying, 'Steve knows my views on him and expense accounts, and I have said it to his face. I've got nothing to hide there. But I have also told him I trust him as a mate and that I know he would not stab me in the back.'

'What a load of bollocks.' Ian said through clenched teeth. I guessed that he thought his attack was foiled because I had not looked at Steve and that it must have come across as if Steve and I had talked about it.

Eventually Steve let out a big sigh. 'Well, I'm not going ahead with all of this without Mike. So if Mike's not in, then it's good night, Vienna.' While I could see that Steve was sticking to the plan, I also felt very uncomfortable. Suddenly, all the pressure was on me as I was now seen to be the bad guy, the one who did not want Ian in and it was my decision whether he stayed or went.

As if to try and reconcile the facts further, I asked Ian, 'So has there been anything else you have done under COMSEC that we should be aware of?'

'Well, there was some work in the Solomon Islands, but that was nothing to do with Iraq' came his reply.

'When was this?' I asked

'Last year,' he replied

'I thought the agreement you and I had regarding COMSEC was that I had a 25 per cent profit share,' I said.

'That was only to do with Algeria,' said Ian.

'So do you mean that all the other meetings I had regarding Nigeria, Brazil, Columbia, Romania, and others would have meant you would not have given me a percentage?' I asked as I leant forward.

'The agreement we had was for Algeria,' said Ian.

'In the beginning it was Algeria, but that was only a small part of it. I spent a huge amount of my time and energy in meetings over many more places, which you were fully aware of, and some would have come off had it not been for your lack of commitment. So I will ask you again. Had anything come of any of the other places, would you have given me a percentage?'

Ian had difficulty maintaining eye contact with me as I fixed my eyes firmly on his. 'It was only Algeria,' he said again.

'Ian, just answer the question, yes or no. If any of the other places, some of which I initiated, came off, would you have given me a percentage? Just yes or no.'

'When it started, we only discussed Algeria,' maintained Ian.

'The agreement was that I was to be the frontman, and at the time it was only Algeria we were looking at. But it very quickly branched into other parts of the world. So were you just going to let me spend all that time and, if anything came off, you would have used the excuse that we started with Algeria, therefore I was not entitled to a percentage? The fact that nothing did come of it is immaterial. For me the fundamental issue is that it appears now that you would have claimed that I was not entitled to a percentage for anything outside of Algeria, even though I had done all the negotiating. So one last time, would you have paid me a percentage on any contracts outside of Algeria?'

'It was Algeria we discussed,' Ian said blankly.

'Well, that's it for me. I am not prepared to go ahead with you in the team, Ian,' I said.

'If Mike's out, then so am I,' Steve said.

'Oh, I see. This was a stitch-up from the beginning,' said Ian, with a reddening face.

To a certain extent he was right. We had gone in there with a predetermined outcome. That did not sit right with me as I have always tried to understand both sides of a story and base my decisions on the evidence. But what I discovered was that Ian's intention was always to stitch me up. So the outcome would have been the same. And that was the end of Ian's involvement.

TRANSITION TO KUWAIT

Steve returned to Kuwait in search of a sponsor. I continued recruiting, and as the weeks rolled by, I began to think it was all a pipe dream. If we could not even get a sponsor in Kuwait, how were we going to operate in Iraq? By mid-September of 2003 I was pretty much resigned to the fact we would not get off first base.

Steve had stumbled across a Lebanese woman by the name of Susan Riley. She was involved in some sort of investment bank but became interested in what we were trying to do and began introducing Steve to some of her clients. There were a few false hopes as potential sponsors carried out due diligence on us but then passed up the opportunity. Then it came. Mishare Al Ghazali, a prominent lawyer and businessman in Kuwait who showed much interest. He ran his own law practice and had his fingers in many pies. Not only was he willing to sponsor us to set up Securiforce International as a Kuwaiti registered company, he was also going to invest half a million dollars to kick-start the whole thing. For his sponsorship and the money, he would be 51 per cent owner of the company under Kuwaiti law but agreed that he, Steve, SO, and I would be 25 per cent profit share. I had no opportunity to discuss this as Steve simply announced he had already agreed, and at the end of the day, I was just glad that we had found a sponsor. With the money available we could also consider paying ourselves a wage and help fund what was turning out to be an expensive exercise in setting up. What I had to do now was to make a final decision on whether to jump ship from a career in the police into what was still a large uncertainty.

I had promised myself that I would not resign from the police until something concrete in the way of a contract came along. But it was also extremely frustrating, sitting in the UK and relying on Steve to push things through. It was agreed that he would chase the business and I would get the operational side set up. I did not want the scenario of a contract being landed and no equipment or men to service it. But there was also a balance to procuring a load of equipment with all the expense before a contract was sorted. I continued to recruit.

By the end of September I made the decision and tendered my resignation. My DCI (detective chief inspector) was shocked, and I later found out there were some senior officers who were pretty pissed off at me resigning and leaving so suddenly. With leave I was owed and overtime I had saved up I effectively left within the week. Not how I would have liked to go, but my gut instinct told me to jump, so I did. It was that inner voice that has rarely steered me wrong in the past.

On the fifth of October I flew out to Kuwait to join Steve and a few others who had been dragged in, like Nigel Bond, who was a former sergeant major from the Royal Anglian Regiment. A quiet sort of guy, surprisingly, for an ex-sergeant major. Steve had come across him working as a security guard at an office building in Cardiff. He was on board to help run the ops side of life and was to be my right-hand man. I would have liked to have recruited this post myself, but on first impressions Nigel filled the role. Then there was Simon Adams. I had known him socially for a few years. He was a former signals sergeant and had spent most of his career in the same regiment as Steve. He was to be a watchkeeper in the ops room. They had flown out to Kuwait a week or so earlier. Not that I knew, as Steve had a habit of doing something and letting me know about it later. Something that mildly pissed me off. Not just because it would have been professional courtesy but also because often it had a cost implication, which often turned out to be a waste. But again I went with it as we needed guys to help do some running around.

With my best suit on I went to meet Mishare. His office was housed within the Kuwaiti Chamber of Commerce, a very nice office with thick pile carpet and a very serene atmosphere. He was an immaculately dressed gentleman in his pristine dishdasha. He came across as quiet but very thorough. His English was not very good, but then again my Arabic was nonexistent. It was clear from the outset that he was purely concerned with the business setup and wanted no involvement in the operational activities of the company. I didn't know what Steve had sold him, but all that mattered was that Mishare had decided to sponsor us and stump up some cash.

For the first few weeks we lived in hotels. This was already burning up a lot of cash, and we needed to find somewhere more permanent and somewhere that would be suitable to set up an ops room and base our activities from. Mishare was very helpful, and we were shown around several villas within Kuwait City. Eventually we settled on a four-story villa in the Jabriya district. The rent was ten thousand dollars a month. It was a bit of a gamble, but we had to adopt the attitude that we were going to succeed and, therefore, should set up accordingly. Otherwise, there was not much point in staying. Steve made a comment that if it all went sour, we could just jump on a plane and head back to the UK and call it a day. My own sense of integrity was a little uneasy with this, but at the end of the day he was right. Sometimes you make investments and they don't always work out.

The villa had a basement, a ground floor that was ideal for the offices and ops room, and then two further floors above which we intended to use as bedrooms for the guys. Apparently this was a typical villa for Kuwait families, where you would find up to four families all living under the one roof as part of the larger family group. Not that it was at all cramped. It was a huge place, complete with a large rear area which would be ideal as a car park.

The next few weeks were spent sorting through all the bureaucracy of registering the company, opening bank accounts, looking for equipment, and all the time networking with the many freight forwarding companies that were also busy setting up. On the twenty-sixth of October 2003 Securiforce International (SFI) was registered.

The same afternoon the company was registered, Steve, SO, and I retired to a nearby Pizza Hut to mull over a few things. The topic of salaries came up. I had not given it much thought but considered that as long as my take-home was slightly better or at least equal to what I had been earning in the police then I would be happy. Once business started rolling in, then we could start to benefit financially. So in my mind I had a figure of around three thousand pounds per month, which would also be tax free. SO began with what appeared to be a pre-planned speech of what he thought Steve and I should be paid. He explained that we had both given up jobs, would be away from our families, and would be the ones doing all the work. He proposed five thousand pounds. One thing I had learnt over the years was the nonresponsive reaction when negotiating. Whatever was offered or proposed, show no reaction so that you keep the other side guessing and hopefully swing the result in your favour. So I remained passive and counted to five. While I counted, I pondered that I was more than happy to receive this sort of money but was also conscious that we had not actually done anything to deserve it. The higher we set our wages, the quicker we would burn up the investment Mishare had given.

I was about to speak when Steve chipped in with 'Seven thousand.' Inwardly, I spluttered, but outwardly, nonresponsive. Steve went on to explain that we were now company directors and that we were going to have to set wages sufficiently high enough for the employees and we should be on more than them. A pretty basic logic, I thought, but a logical one all the same. This would be nearly triple what my take-home had been. I halfheartedly raised concern that it was too high and that we should set a lower salary and reassess once work rolled in and we actually started to turn a profit. After a very short discussion, I capitulated and agreed on the seven. SO then stated that it was agreed and that all three of us should receive the seven thousand. Steve immediately jumped in and explained that it would be him and I that would be doing all the work and going into Iraq and all the other reasons SO had previously raised. SO then offered that his take-home Army salary was four thousand after tax and so he should receive three thousand to make him up to seven. Steve agreed. I also agreed, thinking that SO was not the only one who had been rehearsing their lines.

Now that we had agreed on our salaries, we needed to establish what we were actually going to be billing for our security. We had no idea on how we should cost our services. We began with a simple spreadsheet and added up what we thought it would cost us to employ a guard, fly him over, provide all the equipment and insurance, and feed him. We had to work out whether we would bill on a lump-sum basis or a daily basis. We assessed that a daily basis would be better, as this would cover us in the event of delays caused outside of our control. After many hours of number crunching we settled on a rate of three hundred dollars per man per day as wages for the guys and nine hundred dollars per man per day invoicing rate to clients. This left six hundred dollars per man per day to help cover all the other costs of villa rent, flights, insurance, equipment, and of course, all the non-operational staff. In addition, we also wanted to turn a profit.

From one of our meetings we established a link with

Richard Cromwell, a Scouser who was the country manager for Kuehne + Nagel, a German freight forwarder. He was in his mid-fifties and had spent most of his working life in far-flung corners of the world. He had established an office for Kuehne + Nagel simply as a management setup to coordinate the transportation requirements for KBR (Kellogg, Brown & Root). He would hire trucks from the local market, mostly forty-foot flatbeds which formed convoys, taking material into Iraq for KBR. At any one time he would have over five hundred trucks on the road. At the time, the US Military was providing security, but this was not going to last long, and we wanted to be the preferred supplier of convoy security. Or as the Americans would say, convoy 'mitigation'.

This is where SO came into his own. Being a dry state, alcohol was not easy to come by. But as the defence attaché, SO had a ready supply through the embassy. He had a fully stocked bar in his villa, and Richard was a regular guest. Over a few weeks we got to know Richard well, and apart from him being the country manager, he was also a nice guy. Once we began openly talking about providing security, he was all in favour, but we had two obstacles. One, the US Military was still providing convoy security, and second, KBR's security provider was ArmorGroup. They were by far the largest private security provider in Iraq and had arrived on the shirttails of KBR. But at this stage they were only providing close protection and static guards. The trick was to get Richard to get KBR to agree that Kuehne + Nagel would arrange transport and security as a package.

So began a series of meetings and presentations to various managers within KBR. After each, the various managers appeared delighted with our proposed plan for security. However, on seeing the cost and then picking themselves off the floor, we were then referred up the chain. Our recommendations were that convoys should be no larger than twenty trucks with three escort vehicles. With the sheer number of trucks going up country, the security bill was in the region of one and half million dollars a month. As we got higher up the management chain and my nonresponsive reactions were in full flow, I could feel we were getting closer to the decision-maker. At some point someone had to make a decision, even if the answer was no. At least we could concentrate elsewhere. Late November and into early December the agony of indecision rolled on. Every time we thought we were close, we were referred up again. I could not believe how many levels of management KBR had. Eventually, one of the managers filled out a purchase order, complete with costs, and was about to sign. He paused and said, 'I'll just run this by my line manager.' I could hear a loud scream of 'FOR FUCK'S SAKE JUST SIGN THE BLOODY THING.' Thankfully, it was just inside my head, and I calmly walked away, to return the following day as agreed. My nonresponsive reaction nearly shattered. The following day I returned to be informed that our plan and costs had been referred stateside for authorisation. And so the waiting went on.

Steve had been back to the UK on various meetings, but again with little success. By now we had started to gain info on other private security companies and how they were operating and what their rates were. We were very competitive. In fact, I wondered if we were too cheap and that was why we were not being taken seriously. We saw rates of between one thousand five hundred and two thousand five hundred dollars per man per day. If the KBR project came off, we would need a lot more men than was on my database. Mid December I returned to the UK to continue recruiting. This time I started to receive candidates who had already worked out in Iraq within private security and were looking for better deals. An interview, by definition, is a two-way process, and I was certainly gleaning as much information as possible from these guys. I also had to be extremely careful, as I did not want to let on that SFI had not actually put a boot inside of Iraq. It would not have done our reputation or business development any good at all.

On the sixteenth of December I received a call from Steve. Richard Cromwell had been asked by a Kuehne + Nagel representative in Jordan if he knew of a decent security company that did convoy protection. Like a good chap that he was, he of course replied 'SFI' and put them in touch with Steve. Steve explained that Bechtel were taking some cargo into Iraq from Jordan and that there was to be a meeting in Amman. I was in the UK and Steve was back in Kuwait at this time. I suggested we both went to the meeting as he had the background knowledge of what had already been discussed, and I could pad it out with how we would do it operationally. He then told me that he could not go, as he had to return to the UK. He would not explain why and maintained that I had to go. I was getting a little pissed off by now, as Steve appeared to be doing a lot of running around but not actually achieving much. We had agreed that business development was his show and ops was mine. Going to a meeting to discuss a contract, I thought, fell squarely into business development. And besides, my wedding anniversary was fast approaching, and I had missed a fair few of those over the years due to work. The more I pushed, the more I could tell Steve did not want to go. I thought quickly and decided it was probably better Steve didn't go, as he may well commit SFI to something we did not want. I asked him to e-mail all the info he had.

On the eighteenth of December I received a phone call from James Roberts. He was a project manager with a company called ALE (Abnormal Load Engineering) and was going on the convoy. I was on the escalator in Ikea at the time and nearly fell off when he explained the cargo was a gas turbine and a generator, each weighing 250 tons. They were to be carried on specialist heavy-duty hydraulic trailers and travel at about ten kilometres an hour. My first reaction was, 'Oh shit, Steve, what have you agreed to?' I imagined these large pieces of cargo, the size of a house, crawling through the Iraqi desert and the insurgents casually taking their time to set up an ambush. The thought of 'RPGs for beginners' sprang to mind.

James asked me if two escort vehicles and only six men were going to be enough. I could tell from the way he asked that he didn't think so. I was taken aback, as Steve and I had already discussed that we would never deploy with less than three vehicles. For such a slow-moving target, I quickly assessed that we would require at least five vehicles. I guessed that Steve had already proposed his plan of two vehicles and wondered if changing would jeopardise the potential contract. I tried to regain the situation by stating that Steve had given a general deployment based on faster-moving trucks. We would need to reassess the deployment based on the new information of the size and speed of the convoy. James agreed, and I could sense he appreciated the requirement for a higher level of security. He began talking about flank protection, and I wondered if he was ex-military himself. Later that day he called back and informed me the meeting was to be in Amman on the twentieth and twenty-first of December. I booked a flight for the following day, the nineteenth.

JORDAN MEETING

On the morning of the twentieth of December I joined James for breakfast in the Howard Johnson Hotel, Amman. He was in his late thirties and had a hint of a Yorkshire accent. We chatted briefly about who we were going to see as he had already had several meetings with the potential clients. I established that both SFI and ALE were intended to be subcontractors of Kuehne + Nagel, who in turn were contacted by Bechtel. James immediately made me feel as though we were going in as a team to lay down 'our' plan. Until now I had felt very suspicious of everyone I met and was very guarded about what I said or disclosed. I had never really been involved with multimillion dollar negotiations and really did not know what to expect. But this was it. This was the closest we had got to a contact so far.

We walked a short distance to Kuehne + Nagel's offices and met with Osama Azar. He was the general manager of their Jordan office. He wore a black suit with a black open-neck shirt. He was short and thickset and looked more like a Mafia godfather than anything else. But he had a pleasant nature about him. As we chatted, it appeared to me that both James and Osama were looking to me for a strategy for our meeting with Bechtel. I suppose. After all, the transport side was fairly straightforward, but the security was a key issue. What was pleasing was that our gang was growing, and after only thirty minutes, we set off to the Marriott Hotel to meet with Bechtel as a team. I was growing in confidence all the time.

We assembled in one of the conference rooms and sat around a large table. There were several senior representatives from Bechtel and also some senior US Military Army officers. James gave a short presentation of the transport side of the operations. Osama explained the logistical backup. I gave a short PowerPoint presentation of how SFI planned to protect these pieces, which I had just found out were worth in the region of five to ten million dollars each. No pressure then!

As I was giving my presentation, I was outwardly calm. However, on the inside I was really nervous. Not about giving the presentation. I was confident that the tactics and intended operational aspects were well thought through, and modesty aside, I thought I sounded professional. What I was worried about was if the military guys started asking questions about specific locations within Iraq. I would have nothing to base an answer on, and it would have been quickly apparent that everything I was giving was based on theory and not on proven track record. I countered such questions stating that 'confirmatory' reconnaissance would be needed for particular points on the route. I also assessed that it was highly likely that these senior officers had not actually been out on the ground and would not want to highlight their own lack of knowledge. Whatever the reason, no such questions were forthcoming, and any discussions were limited to what the interface would be between the military and private security. A liaison officer would be allocated to travel with the convoy. The key point for me was that all agreed that the security would be five escort vehicles and a total of twenty men. From the meeting it was also established that a full route survey would be needed to assess the viability of the route in relation to the weight and dimensions of the turbine and generator.

The final aspect was the commercial side. Final figures had not been passed to Bechtel by Osama, and it was agreed that we would meet the following afternoon to confirm rates. I now had a much better understanding of what was required and turned my thoughts to what rates I would put in. I was conscious that if I submitted daily rate for when the guys were in Iraq, SFI could get stung for standby days for delays outside our control. We would have to pay our guys regardless but would not be able to charge for days when the convoy was not actually deployed. In a flash of inspiration I decided to submit a rate of $900 per man per day for inside Iraq and a rate of $600 per man per day outside of Iraq while on standby. Osama appeared pleased with the proposal.

That night over a few beers I chatted with James. He was not ex-military but had been brought up mostly in Germany, as his father was based there in the Army. He had lived in Abu Dhabi for the past ten years and had been involved with heavy lift transport for longer. I pondered that we had based our planning on convoy protection, but now we were going to have to provide security for a person doing a route survey from the Jordanian border to the Al Quds Power Station in the northern suburbs of Baghdad. It all suddenly felt more real. After far too many beers I went to bed with my mind still racing.

The following afternoon we reassembled in the conference room. Just before we all sat down, Osama took me to one side and informed me that all the rates had been submitted and would not be discussed in the meeting. But if asked, I was to refer to him. I guessed that he had also put his markup on our security. I was not fussed, as long as the markup was not too big and stopped the whole thing. The meeting was very short, and the only thing I wanted was a start date. I was conscious that in a Muslim country and with military on an operational tour, not much thought would be given to the fact Christmas was upon us. I envisaged trying to deploy guys from the UK over Christmas and also trying to get together the equipment we needed. However, a start date was not given, and I returned to the UK on the twenty-second of December with an agreement on our rates but not an actual signed contract. I maintained to Osama that we would need six days for mobilisation but would not even begin to move without a signed contract.

SCRAMBLE TO THE START LINE

I returned to the UK just in time for Christmas. In between the turkey and pudding I was checking my e-mails. I was expecting an e-mail from Osama, giving notification of deployment. I had no idea when it would come, as no indication had been given in Amman. On the morning of the twenty-sixth of December Steve called me and told me he had just received a fax through from Osama with a signed order. We were off and running. After dancing a little jig, I called Nigel and told him to pack, as we were on the night flight to Kuwait.

Simon picked me up midafternoon and drove Nigel and me to Heathrow Airport. En route I started phoning the list of guys. Of the fifty or so guys on the database, I managed to get ten who were ready to go. It was between Christmas and New Year, and it was not looking good. I had e-mailed the list to Steve and asked him to continue phoning around while I would be on the overnight flight to Kuwait. We were to meet James at the Jordan/Iraq border on the third of January 2004 to commence a route survey. It would take two days to travel across Iraq from Kuwait, which gave us seven days. Seven days to mobilise a team, procure vehicles, weapons, ammunition, body armour, and radios.

Vehicles – We had visited several car showrooms in Kuwait and had decided on Nissan Patrols. They were 4.8 litre 4×4s, and we had primed the manager for short-notice delivery. There had been much debate over soft-skinned vehicles versus armoured vehicles. The standard B6 armoured vehicle would protect against small-arms fire but would not protect against roadside bombs or RPG (rocket-propelled grenades). They also tended to be rather heavy and not much use for off-road. We would need to be able to go off-road to provide a security cordon around the convoy.

Another factor was that on most B6 armoured vehicles, the windows would not wind down. If the vehicle was disabled, you would not be able to return fire and then exit the vehicle. You would have to potentially step out into a hail of bullets.

Body armour – We had also identified a supplier of body armour in the UK who had shipped over two hundred sets to Kuwait. An agreement was reached that we could have some at short notice, but they were still trapped in Kuwaiti Customs at the time.

Radios – Dean Jones was an ex-Army mate who was now working in the communications world. He had advised on the best vehicle-mounted radios and also for man-portable radios. We had also arranged Thyria satellite phones as there was no mobile phone coverage in Iraq. He had been primed to secure enough comms equipment and be ready to fly out to Kuwait to fit them into the vehicles, which we were still to procure.

Weapons – This was a real worry. While I had been in the UK recruiting and also to Jordan, Steve had been speaking to an officer in the Kuwaiti Army. He had been introduced by SO and had offered to source us with AK-47s. However, he was proving to be unreliable. The only legitimate source of weapons in Kuwait was through a gun shop owned by one of the sheiks. Again SO's connections came in useful, as he knew him. I asked SO to arrange a meeting between the sheik and Mishare, as it would have to be a Kuwaiti who was to buy them.

By the time we reached Heathrow, I had at least some of the guys on their way, the vehicles ordered, Dean warned off to bring the radios out, and the body armour earmarked. Holy shit, this was going to be tight.

We landed early the next morning, the twenty-seventh of December. The time difference to the UK was four hours, so I didn't expect to get Steve on the phone. However, a text dropped in on turning on my mobile. We had another three guys on board. That made a total of fourteen guys so far, including Nigel.

Back at the villa I started e-mailing and calling more guys. I needed twenty men for the job, so including myself and Nigel, I needed another eighteen. There were fourteen confirmed and on their way for tonight's flight, so only another four to get. I called SO, and he confirmed a meeting was arranged that evening between Mishare and the sheik at his gun shop in downtown Kuwait. I was also to attend.

At about 7:00 pm that evening Nigel and myself met with Mishare in a car park to the rear of the gun shop, not far from the Chamber of Commerce building. We went in, and immediately my heart sank. I was not expecting to see a full arsenal that Rambo would be proud of, but I had envisaged a little more than there was. I quickly scanned the shop and could see a variety of what looked like target air pistols and few rifles that looked no larger than .22 calibre. I could see nothing that would be remotely suitable for what we wanted. We went into a back room and sat with Mishare and the sheik. No English was spoken, and for about ten minutes it appeared as if pleasantries were being exchanged between the two Kuwaitis. Nigel sat, wide eyed, and appeared overawed by what was going on. I was listening intently to see if I could pick up anything that may have referred to weapons. Not that I could speak or understand Arabic, but I thought I may have heard something. Alas, I heard nothing that led me to believe we were going to be in luck.

After about the third cup of tea, we got up to leave. Or at least I thought we were going to leave. As we walked back through to the main shop, a male called Fred (whose real name will remain secret for obvious reasons) pulled back a curtain to reveal a door. We walked through and went down a flight of steps to a basement. My heart began to race, thinking we were about to be shown what we had really come to see. We emerged into a room about ten metres by six metres. On all walls were glass cabinets, and down the centre of the room, a low-level glass cabinet. On the walls I could see only what appeared to be bolt-action hunting rifles. They were very nice, but I wanted assault rifles. In the low-level cabinet I could see a mix of pistols. The closest thing there to what we wanted was a Taurus 9 millimetre semi-automatic pistol. Effectively, it was a Brazilian-manufactured pistol very similar to the 9 millimetre Browning used by the British Army. For convoy protection they were next to useless, and if I ever needed to use one, then something would have seriously gone wrong. But I thought that I had better buy some. Firstly, to satisfy Mishare that his efforts had not been wasted, and secondly, it was all we had.

The sheik agreed to sell four pistols and a total of one hundred rounds of 9 millimetre ammunition. Mishare had to buy them, being the Kuwaiti, and it was agreed that they would be taken direct to the border and into Iraq. Mishare and the sheik headed upstairs to sort out payment.

'OK, my friend, what else do you have?' I asked Fred, with a knowing wink of my eye.

I noticed Fred's eye flash to the door leading upstairs. I knew there was more. But then I suddenly felt a slight panic as I contemplated some dodgy arms deal going down. But nothing ventured, nothing gained. I tried again.

'I'm really looking for something a bit more than a couple of pistols. I really need military-style rifles,' I pushed.

'We do not have any,' Fred replied, with what I thought was emphasis on the we.

Fred was looking a little nervous, and we could hear some movement from upstairs. He packed the four pistols into a box and headed upstairs. Nigel and I followed him up. Mishare and the sheik shook hands, and we headed out of the shop. Mishare bid good night and quickly left. I felt he was uneasy about the whole thing and wanted to put distance between himself and two Brits with illegally possessed weapons in the centre of Kuwait. As we got into our Land Cruiser, Fred approached and handed me a business card.

'Perhaps you call me a little later,' he muttered and headed back into the shop.

'Starbucks?' I asked Nigel as we drove away.

After a cappuccino and a muffin, I called Fred's mobile. It was now after ten at night. After several rings Fred answered. I dispensed with any small talk and went straight to the point.

'Fred, I'm looking for someone who can get me some descent weapons I can use in Iraq for security work?' I asked. There was a slight pause.

'I have some FAL' came the reply.

'OK,' I said. 'Anything else?' I had no idea what a FAL was, but I did not want to end things before I had exhausted all possibilities.

'I also have MP5,' he replied. Now I knew what they were: a 9 millimetre semi-automatic carbine. I had fired one on a range many times, and it is the weapon you will see the police handling at most airports in the UK. Ideal for use in a vehicle, as it is a relatively short weapon and effective to about 100 metres.

After some waltzing about, we agreed to meet in the car park near the gun shop an hour later. I asked Nigel if he knew what a FAL was, but despite being an infantryman, he had never heard of it. Just before midnight we pulled into the car park and parked alongside an old Toyota pickup. Fred got out and pulled aside a tarpaulin in the back. It was dark, with very little street lighting. I half expected a burst of police sirens and to be arrested, but all remained quiet. I looked into the back of the pickup and could see the MP5 and an AK-47. I reached down and started checking the working parts of the MP5, and Nigel did likewise with the

AK-47. Both appeared in good condition.

'So where is the FAL?' I asked. Fred pulled the tarp further across, and to my surprise, I was looking at what I knew as an SLR (self-loading rifle). This was identical to the standard British Army rifle that both Nigel and I were very familiar with. In my humble opinion, a brilliant weapon. The British Army was just changing over to the SA80 rifle at the time I was leaving — and by all accounts, a better rifle — but I liked the SLR, and I knew that a lot of the guys I had recruited were old school and would also want to get their hands on one.

Before Nigel had a chance, I picked up the FAL and checked it over. It was in mint condition and also had a fully automatic function. The SLR we knew were only semi-automatic, but what I knew as the Belgium FN had the full auto setting. So the FAL was actually the real monty, an FN. It was ideal. I was conscious that buying these weapons illegally was going to be very expensive. I tried to be cool towards the FN so as not to let on I was very interested in them.

'OK, Fred, how many of the MP5 and AKs do you have, and how much?' I asked.

'I have two of the MP5 and three of the AK,' replied Fred.

'How much MP5?' I asked.

'MP5 six hundred dollar and AKs five hundred,' offered Fred in more of a question.

'You're having a laugh, I would say more like four hundred for the MP5 and three hundred for the AKs.' I quickly rebutted, as if I knew what I was on about. The truth was that I have never bought a weapon before and would not have a clue where to start. But like everything in the Middle East, I was sure you could barter.

'Five hundred for the MP5 and four hundred for the AK,' Fred came back with, after a moment of thought. So I could see he was open to negotiation. It was the FNs I was really interested in.

'OK. Let me have a think.' I paused a second and then asked, 'How much for the FAL?'

'Five hundred,' said Fred.

'I'm not really interested in them. Can you get any more AKs and MP5s?' I asked, steering interest away from the FALs.

'I will try, but this is all I have now,' replied Fred, just as a set of headlights swung into the car park and then left. Fred quickly pulled the tarpaulin back over his cache of weapons. It gave a second or two of thinking time.

'How many FALs do you have?' I asked, guessing that Fred would find it a lot harder to find a market for these over AKs and MP5s.

'I have six of these,' he said.

'With magazines for all of these?' I asked.

'Yes, of course,' replied Fred.

'And how many rounds can you get?' I asked.

'I will have to see, but they are a dollar a round,' Fred said in a far more firm manner, letting me know that was not open to negotiation. I turned and muttered to Nigel as if we were discussing the deal.

'OK, Fred, I'll tell you what I will do. I will take both MP5s for five hundred each, the three AKs for four hundred each. And I will take the six FALs for three hundred each. Maybe I can sell them on in Iraq,' I offered.

After a moment of thought Fred agreed, and he said he would call me the following evening to arrange handover and payment. At least there was now the promise of eleven weapons, and we had four pistols.

Nigel and I drove out of the car park and headed back to the villa. It was nearly two in the morning, and we had an early pickup at the airport for the first batch of guys flying out from the UK. I didn't sleep much that night.

Bright and early the next morning we headed for the airport to collect the guys who had flown out overnight. As they emerged from arrivals I could not help but wonder if all would also be going back safely. It was a sobering thought and made it all the more real.

I then turned my attention to vehicles. Mishare had a contact who had offered two 4×4 armoured vehicles. However, when we collected them, one was an old shitty Land Cruiser, and as I had suspected, the windows would not open. The other was a Jeep Cherokee. Both had been adapted and not purpose built. The suspension had not been beefed up, and the door hinges could barely support the weight of the doors. I visited the Nissan dealer again and ordered five Nissan Patrols. Despite being reassured he could supply within two days, he now informed me they would take five days. I would have to take the two armoured 4×4 from Mishare's mate.

My main concern regarding vehicles was that we had two for the initial recce and at least Dean could fit the radios to the two armoured vehicles when he arrived on the next day's flight with all the radios.

Early afternoon I called in to see Mishare to collect some cash for tonight's arms deal. He casually opened a draw to his desk and handed me a large handful of dollars, asking me if thirty thousand was enough. I glanced into the draw and could see that it was full of cash. I assured him it was sufficient for tonight.

Late afternoon I called Fred, and after several attempts to reach him I was beginning the think it was not going to happen. But then about ten that night Fred called. Nigel and I headed off for the same car park. As we approached the vicinity of the car park, I had an uneasy feeling. We stopped a block away and took a walk to have a look around the area to see if anything looked out of place. I had contemplated the possible punishment of being caught with illegal weapons in Kuwait. Hanging was not that appealing.

All looked OK, so in we went. Fred was waiting with one other guy. I was not sure who was more nervous. Me, Fred, or Nigel. Not wanting to waste any time, we quickly set about checking over the other weapons. All looked good, and there were two magazines per weapon.

'How many rounds for each?' I asked Fred.

'I have one thousand rounds of 9 millimetres, three hundred rounds for the AKs, and only two hundred rounds for the FALs,' rattled off Fred. I was disappointed with the lack of rounds for the FALs, but beggars could not be choosers.

As I was counting out the cash, I could hear in the distance a police siren. It was way off in the distance, and I did not think it was heading our way but again focused the mind on what we were doing. The deal done, we cross loaded the weapons into the back of our vehicle. Fred agreed to call me if any further weapons came his way and especially any further rounds.

As we pulled out of the car park Nigel, and I both burst out laughing. Holy shit, we had just secured some weapons! The last intelligence package I had dealt with as a Detective Sergeant in Gwent Police was for a local lad who was allegedly bringing weapons back from Holland hidden under his car in a tube, just like Edward Fox in the film Day of the Jackal. Now here I was, doing some dodgy arms deal in some dark Kuwaiti car park. Oh, if my old DI could have seen me now!

We got back to the villa, and a buzz went round as the weapons were brought in. Shep had prepared a room in the basement of the villa as an armoury, complete with racks. Obviously, we should not have had illegally possessed weapons in Kuwait, never mind an armoury in the basement. But we had no alternative, as we didn't have a base in Iraq and we wanted to be based in Kuwait to try and corner the market in convoy protection. It was just ironic that our first job was to come out from Jordan.

The following day, the twenty-ninth of December, I visited KNY (Kuwait New York) Logistics Company with one of the new lads, Kerry Jones. He was an ex-sergeant from the RRW (Royal Regiment of Wales). This was where the body armour should have been. However, we were told that the body armour and helmets were still stuck in customs. I needed forty sets as we had agreed to supply for the ALE crew as well. I phoned Steve, who was still in UK, and got the UK-based company to fax a letter to KNY Logistics to provide paperwork to me so that I could try another way to get customs clearance. Their rep stated they had been trying for over three months and scoffed when I said I would get it sorted.

I was aware SO knew the head of Kuwaiti Customs. So I faxed him the paperwork and a bottle of whiskey. Later the body armour was released. This all took about two hours, and the KNY Rep could not believe it. I casually stated it was no problem and that we knew people in high places—the perks of having the British defence attaché on board. I was lining up the ducks, and one by one they were being knocked off. Vehicles, weapons, ammunition, body armour, and comms sorted. The one thing I still didn't have and could not get my hands on was maps. We had even tried our contacts in the US Military, and they also had problems getting maps.

SO had managed to get a few maps for the Basra area, as this was the British sector. I called around his place to collect them on the morning of thirty-first December. He appeared slightly sozzled even at that time, and then he explained he had just found out he had been awarded a CBE in the New Year's honours list. He was going to have a bash at his residence that night to celebrate that and, of course,

New Year's Eve. He invited me, but I had not slept much for the past week, and the following day I would be leading the first mission into Iraq. The thought of doing that with a hangover prevented me from accepting, which was unlike me to turn down a party.

That night, Steve was also flying out to Kuwait with more guys. However, we were still one short to make up the twenty needed.

I had chosen the team to go on the recce. In the front vehicle with me were Dominic Grey, the headshot ex-para, and Kerri Jones. In the rear vehicle would be Nigel, Ray Clark, and Gareth Evans. Both Ray and Gareth had served together in the Royal Marines and had since both been police officers in South Wales Police. Perhaps I had a bias towards ex-military/police guys. We spent the rest of the day packing the vehicles, expecting to be out on the road for the next ten days.

The first of January 2004, and the recce team assembled outside the armoury. Shep dished out the weapons and ammunition. There was not much talking going on as we loaded the rounds into the magazines and completed the final packing of the vehicles. It was still dark outside as I wanted to complete the hour's drive to the border to cross at daybreak, to give the maximum daylight to travel up to Baghdad.

'Cheers, Shep, see you in about a week,' I said as he extended his hand to shake mine.

'Stay low, move fast, trust no one,' Shep said in a sombre and firm voice. He had been around the block a bit, and I guess it was the closest he could get to telling me to be careful without being too emotional. He turned and walked inside.

The drive to the border was uneventful, and just before dawn, we arrived. Just short of the border crossing point was a small complex of portacabins manned by the US

Military. I went in and handed over my fake MOD (Ministry of Defence) contractors pass and completed the trip ticket. The sergeant behind the desk duly stamped it, and the first of many blags was complete. Back at the vehicles the guys were donning their body armour. The weapons remained out of sight.

As we drove to the crossing point, daylight was just breaking. The Kuwaiti soldiers simply watched as we drove slowly past their checkpoint. Reclined back on a chair, they definitely gave the impression they could not give a shit about what we were doing or where we were going. A hundred metres further on we came to the US Military checkpoint. I handed over the trip ticket, and we were waved into no man's land between the borders. As we transited the kilometre between the borders I could see on the other side of the road a series of lanes where vehicles coming out of Iraq were lined up and being searched. I thought that would be interesting when we returned.

As we approached the checkpoint at the Iraqi border, the mood was different. At the Kuwait side the US Military had soft hats and weapons slung. Here, weapons were held and helmets worn. It was clear we were entering a whole new ball game. As we passed through, the soldier gave a halfhearted salute. I just nodded in acknowledgement. About a hundred metres past the checkpoint we pulled into a large open area and got out.

'OK, guys, tool up,' I said. From under the seats the hidden weapons were produced and loaded. We did not hang around, as I believed that movement was always going to be our best defence, and soon we were off. I was driving the front vehicle and Ray the rear vehicle. Before we had time to contemplate too much we were entering the small village of Safwan. Despite the early hour, the kids were out running along the side of the road, rubbing their stomachs, and putting their fingers to their lips, hoping we would throw them some food. The drill was not to give anything to avoid attracting more and potentially blocking the road. The speed increased, and we were out the other side of the village a short time later. The road was single track and had many potholes. I was conscious that with the added weight of the armour and all the kit we had, the tyres would be vulnerable to potholes.

About a kilometre further we reached the main highway heading north. The military had named this route Tamper, and I had been briefed to simply follow the tac (tactical) signs all the way to BIAP (Baghdad International Airport), about four hundred and fifty kilometres away. As we left the single track onto the six-lane highway, a couple of American Humvees sat guard at the junction.

As we headed north, we had three lanes our side of the central reservation, and there were three lanes the other side. To either side of Tamper, it was flat open ground but with many small buildings dotted about. I could also see the odd person wandering around.

I took a moment to ponder the situation. I was leading a team of five other guys into probably the most hostile country in the world, and to be honest, we were not fully prepared. We had a fair mix of weapons, but not a lot of ammunition. We had the rest of the kit, but no maps. The ones we did have were for Basra, and we were skimming the outskirts and heading north. We had GPS, but that just told us where we were at any given point. All I had was a verbal brief of following Tamper until we saw a sign to our right for BIAP. There would be two staging posts en route at Camps Cedar and Scannia. There we could refuel, and if progress had been delayed, we could stay overnight in a secure location. But we had to be at the Jordanian border on the morning of the third of January, and we needed to reach BIAP this first night. To me it was like heading into the unknown. I had no idea really what to expect and felt anxious for the other guys. I was not worried about me. This was my company, and I was going to earn big bucks, if it all worked out. OK. I know these guys had signed up voluntarily and were being paid well, but I still questioned whether I could have done more to reduce the risk of any of them being killed or seriously injured. I looked across at Dom. There was glint in his eye and a grin on this face. He was already loving it.

And the banter started. Piss taking between the paras and the marines. Or the 'Meat and Veg' for the para reg and the 'Cabbage Patch' for the marines and their green berets.

We had not gone more that about ten kilometres when there was a bang. A blown tyre. We must have hit a pothole. I managed to keep the wagon under control and bring it to a stop on the hard shoulder. Shit, I could not believe it. We had just started, and this had now happened. It was exactly this sort of scenario that I was concerned about, being stationary and vulnerable on the side of the road. But this is where our preplanning came in handy, as we had practiced tyre changing. Lookouts were posted, and within ten minutes we were on our way again. A Formula 1 pit team would have been proud. But I was concerned that we only had a couple of spares for each wagon, and if we were to get flats on a regular basis, we would be screwed.

As we headed for BIAP I carried out regular checks over the radio on fuel consumption. We were all constantly scanning the roadside and overhead bridges for movement. Those we did see appeared to be getting on with their own business and not too interested in us. We were maintaining about 140 kilometres per hour, and progress was good. We passed a few military convoys which had a heavy security presence. We also overtook several civilian convoys which had no security and were over a kilometre in length, containing up to fifty trucks.

By late morning we were approaching Camp Cedar,

our first refuelling point. Both wagons were still half full, but best practice was to refuel on every possible occasion. Up ahead I could see that the road was full of trucks and a lot of military. At first I thought there had been an attack but then realised it was the queue to get into Cedar. A soldier waved us through and informed us they had run out of fuel but there was some at Camp Scannia. Although we were not inside the camp, there was a heavy US Military presence, so we pulled over for a leg stretch. After a couple of minutes, we assessed we would have enough fuel to reach Camp Scannia, so we decided to crack on.

Leaving the mass of trucks behind, we continued on, and as we did, we soon ran out of road. The signs for Tamper directed us onto a dust track. I could see that there was road construction ongoing. The dirt track was graded and relatively smooth, but speed was reduced, and I guessed our fuel consumption would increase. We continued more or less in a straight line for about one hundred kilometres on the track. Every now and again there would be a few kilometres of tarmac with a number of construction vehicles busily adding to the road. Eventually back on hard top road again, we picked up the speed, but the Land Cruiser had been very thirsty, and it was close to sucking fumes. We had decided against carrying jerry cans on or in the vehicles due to the potential fire hazard if we got hit by a roadside bomb. What we had in the tanks was all we had. I knew Camp Scannia was not far ahead, but luck was not on our side, as Ray came over the radio and informed me they were out of fuel. I could see in the rear-view mirror they were pulling over. I quickly spun our wagon around and headed back. Either side of the highway, it was fairly built up, and I could see a lot of people. On the rooftop about two hundred metres away I could see two males, each with what appeared to be AKs. They just stood there and did not appear to be doing anything. Again, in preparation, we had towlines attached and quickly hooked up Ray's wagon. I just hoped we had enough fuel to tow it to Camp Scannia.

It was about midafternoon, and we reached Camp Scannia. Compared to Cedar, it was relatively quiet, and we were waved straight in by the gate sentry. We followed the signs to the fuel point, and a little Filipino guy came out from a hut and handed me a millboard. I could see that it was for contractors and mostly were listed KBR (Kellogg, Brown and Root). We were not officially entitled to get fuel as we did not have a contract with US Aide, the overall contractor for rebuilding Iraq. But I had been briefed by my US Military contact to just fill it in under KBR. The military were not really interested in hampering private security companies, and they helped lessen the burden on their resources. We refuelled and headed off. We had about a hundred and fifty kilometres to go and about three hours of daylight left to reach BIAP. I wanted to arrive in daylight, especially when navigating through Baghdad for the first time.

As we again headed north and towards Baghdad, I could see an increase in the number of burnt-out vehicles on the roadside and the number of bomb craters. You could feel the heightened alert state within the team. More chatter over the radio about seen movement and a firmer grip on the weapons. Then up ahead, a soldier out on foot waving us down. I could see a line of military vehicles stationary on the inside lane. We approached slowly and came to a stop just in front of the soldiers, who were all pointing their M4 rifles at us. On seeing white faces they lowered their weapons, and one approached. He informed us there had been an IED up ahead and it would take a while to clear. So we dismounted and waited. After two hours we saw movement, and we again headed off. I was conscious that we were overtaking a large US Military convoy which had been stationary for over two hours. If I were a bad guy, I would have had plenty of time to set up another ambush up ahead. We had to crack on as we were going to run out of daylight. I also guessed that if there were another IED waiting, they would go for the slower-moving convoy rather than two faster-moving vehicles. Or at least that was what I hoped. It was pretty much what the British Army had adopted in Northern Ireland over the years. Try to make yourself a less attractive target than the next one.

As darkness fell we were just approaching the outskirts of Baghdad. There were a number of intersections on the highway, but there were very few road signs. Most had been removed during the invasion. I had been told that the sign for BIAP had been spray painted on the side of a building just off the road on the right-hand side. Not the best directions but all we had. I knew we were on a stretch of road where most attacks happened, and being in two nice shiny 4×4, we stuck out like a sore thumb. I also knew BIAP was to the west of the city, and we did not need to go through the city to get to it.

'The airport!' Dom shouted, giving me a bit of a fright and pointing to a small sign hanging off one of the overhead gantries. I guessed it would lead to the airport and most probably on main roads all the way in. But that was where I was wrong. In no time at all we were on minor roads in the suburbs of Baghdad. It was like rush hour anywhere else in the world, and we were gridlocked in heavy traffic. I could also see many people walking along the roads and paying us far too much attention for my liking. I thought the best option was to get back out onto the highway and try again for the sign.

'Follow me,' I said over the radio and turned sharp left, mounting the pavement and crossing over to the other side. Thankfully the tyres withstood it, and we quickly headed back out onto the highway. We continued on as the highway turned westward and ran along the southern edge of Baghdad. After about ten kilometres, there, in spray paint on the side of the building, was a 'BIAP' with a large arrow pointing down a side road. Simple but effective. We turned off and, after about three kilometres, approached a checkpoint. I could make out a tank and a couple of Humvees in the darkness. We slowed and turned to side lights. A soldier greeted us, and looking at my MOD contractors pass, he waved us in. We were now in BIAP, a secure location to the west of Baghdad.

We followed the signs for the contactor's camp and found some tented accommodation. We set up out cots and headed over to the DEFAC (dining facility). Again our contractors pass gained us entry, and inside were several hundred US Military. A few gave us a glance, but most went about eating their food. You can always rely on the US Military setting up excellent catering for their troops. After some scoff we headed over to the PX (post exchange, the US equivalent of the NAAFI). We spent about half an hour looking around. Nigel and I were just walking out, chatting, when suddenly there was an explosion about a hundred metres away, out across the car park in the direction of our vehicles. I guessed a mortar round. I was aware Ray and Gareth had headed out before us. After about a minute and no further explosions, we also went out. About twenty-five metres away from our vehicles I could see a scuff mark in the car park and a couple of soldiers looking at what I assumed was the point of impact. As we walked towards the vehicles, I could see Ray sitting in the driver's seat and Gareth in the passenger seat. Both were eating M&Ms.

'All right, guys?' I enquired.

'Yeah, just a mortar over by there,' replied Gareth, shovelling in another mouthful.

'Oh, that's OK, then,' I said in a matter of fact way and climbed into our wagon.

We headed back to the tents. I called Steve back in the

ops room in Kuwait and gave a full update over the sat phone. Two of the guys did not get the flight, so we were still three short for the main team. After checking the shower facilities, there was little to do, so we turned in for the night. As I lay on my cot I reflected on the first day. Not quite your normal day in the office. I was happy so far.

Before first light we were back in the DEFAC and wafting down a hearty breakfast. As we ate I could hear in the distance more explosions. Again, probably mortars. Four or five. And they sounded like they were getting closer. After each muffled crack, there would be a slight pause in the conversation. I looked around, and the several hundred US soldiers appeared oblivious to them. Then one a lot closer, and the building shuddered a little; a second or two of silence, and again on with routine.

'Dawn chorus,' chuckled Dom in between shovelling in mouthfuls of hash browns and beans.

At first light we were lined up at the exit, waiting to leave. The road we were heading out onto was a highway heading directly west to the Jordanian border and would pass Fallujah and Ramadi, two of the worst hot spots. I reset the trip metre, and we pulled out. We were out before any of the convoys had started, so the road was relatively clear. The Iraqis still did not have access to many cars, and the ones that were on the road were slow and in poor condition. As we passed Fallujah, to our left the roadside was littered with all sorts of debris. Old burnt-out tyres and vehicles. Lots of hiding placed for roadside IEDs. We kept in the centre lane and maintained a high speed. As we passed Ramadi, the highway crossed over the Euphrates River. The road bridge was about two hundred metres across, and I was not so sure that would take the 250 ton cargo we would be bringing this way. We quickly pulled over to take some photos. I could see that running across the river, down below the main bridge, was an old steel bridge. It looked rickety and would also mean having to come off the main highway through Ramadi itself to get to.

As we left Ramadi behind us, we headed off across the Western Desert. There was a lot of nothing there, and the road headed in a straight line. To both sides was flat open desert, and every few kilometres there was an overbridge which went from nowhere to nowhere. But I assumed each one would be too low for our cargo, so we would most likely have to travel on the old Route 10 that ran along in the same direction. We maintained a steady speed to conserve fuel. We had bought a couple of jerry cans at BIAP. Lessons learnt!

We made good progress, and after 553 kilometres we arrived at the FOB (forward operating base) at the Jordanian border. I had previously made contact with the captain there and arranged for us to be able to stay within their secure perimeter overnight. Not that it was that secure, and anyone could have thrown a grenade right across the whole compound — it was that small. We were shown to our accommodation: a piece of corridor in one of the buildings. At least it was indoors. Because as we had headed west, we had been climbing gradually the whole time and were now at a higher altitude, and it was going to be cold at night.

I managed to pick up the Jordanian mobile network, so I called Steve. We were now only one short, and the rest of the guys were busy preparing kit and training. I also called James Roberts from ALE, who was now in Jordan and would cross over the border at first light the next day. Not much to do, we had another early night.

ROUTE SURVEY

Just after 8:00 am and having scraped ice of the windscreens, we were sat just inside the Iraq side of the border. James had called on the mobile and informed me he was under immigration process to get in. About thirty minutes later he came strolling across the border. He had an exaggerated walk that John Cleese and the Ministry of Funny Walks would have been proud of. His kit was in a holder, and he looked more like he was going for a sleep over at his mate's house. He had a big grin on his face and greeted us with 'Well, that was fun getting through that bunch of Muppets.'

I gave him a set of body armour and a helmet, and we chatted over the plan for the day. We were to make our way along the old road parallel to the main highway. The route would take us through a small village of Ar Rutbah and onwards towards Ramadi. The intention was to meet up with a group at a given location approximately 80 kilometres west of Ramadi. The group would consist of Major Joe Anger (great name) from the US Corps of Engineers, Captain Davina French, who would be our liaison officer, and a couple of guys from the Iraqi Ministry of Electricity. Then we would complete the route on into Baghdad to the Green Zone.

So we started on our first real op. A route survey with a client, whose safety and protection was in our hands.

At first, progress was slow, as we stopped at every culvert and overhead wire for James to take measurements. After an hour, we had only made 20 kilometres.

'Fuck this,' said James. 'We'll take forever at this rate. We'll only stop if it looks dodgy.'

On the old road we saw very few vehicles. It was

about ten metres wide and in good condition. There were also lots of culverts, and all would have to be checked. Only visually, as there would not be enough time to complete a full check for IEDs. There were good fields of view, and I envisaged that when we were crawling along with the turbine and generator, we would have plenty of time to keep a moving cordon to ensure no surprises. In the open this was going to be easy. Buildup areas would be a whole new ball game.

After about an hour we approached Ar Rutbah. Our intended route was to take us right through the village. Windows down and weapons made ready. We pulled into the village and stopped short of a small bridge running over a dry ditch. During the rain, this would fill. The bridge was badly damaged and would need a lot of work. James strode around and assessed the viability. The locals all stopped what they were doing and watched. The security team was spread out, watching, continually moving. There were adult males with AKs either slung over their shoulder or just held down by their sides. None looked threatening. The guys nodded and smiled at the locals. Many responded positively. Despite this being our first actual interaction with the Iraqi people while on an op, the atmosphere was relaxed, and my spider senses were calm. After several minutes of leaping about and generally putting on a bit of a show for the local kids, James declared we would have to find another route.

Prior to entering the village, I had seen a road to the left heading back to the main highway. I guessed there would be a route back to the old road perhaps the other side of the village. We doubled back, and with much friendly waving to the locals, we retraced our route back out of the village and turned towards the highway. Thankfully, there was a route that took us back to the old road and totally circumvented the village.

At times the old road ran alongside the highway but

at other times were a few kilometres away. After only thirty minutes, leaving Ar Rutbah behind us, bang! And another blown tyre on the Cherokee. Only one spare left. I did not fancy continuing on with no further spares and no idea whether we could repair or replace them. After some thought, I decided to send the Cherokee back to the FOB at the Jordanian border. Dom, Kerry, and Gareth would go back with one of the punctured tyres and see if they could get it fixed at a garage which we had seen near the border. Nigel, Ray, me, and along with James, would continue on. We would also take the second punctured tyre and see if we could get it fixed in Baghdad. I was not keen to separate the two vehicles, but the only option was to risk going on and being stuck with another blown tyre or abandon the mission. I made the judgement call based on a simple run along the highway back to the border for Dom and his crew and that we would soon be linking up with others. Dom was to call me as soon as he reached the border.

After a few hours we approached the coordinates given by Captain Davina French. The name sounded hot, and the guys were all rather excited to meet up with her. As we approached, I could see several more vehicles than I was expecting. I could see what appeared to be about twelve Iraqi males with AKs in a sort of perimeter around some white people. They were smartly dressed, so I did not think they were insurgents, but all the same it was not what we were expecting. Someone in US Military uniform waved us in. From the general stance, I could tell this was a female. Presumably Davina.

We got out, and introductions were made. The bunch of Iraqis were allegedly former Saddam bodyguards and had been contracted by the Ministry of Electricity. However, their team leader was a Brit.

'Hi, I'm Jock, and this bunch of "eejits" are supposed to be my team,' he exclaimed in a broad Jock accent and rolling his eyes. I guess he was right, considering they were supposed to be security and all of them were facing inwards with their backs to any potential threat that may approach. On the contrary my SFI guys were spread out and scanning the distance. There was a lot of activity about five hundred metres away at what appeared to be a service station.

Joe Anger was a tall chap in his late thirties. Davina was a slight woman also in her late thirties. Standing quietly in the background was an older man in military uniform. He was Sergeant Major Frank Something-or-Other and a veteran of everything the US Military has started and not finished during the twentieth century. He was like an amalgamation of all the sergeant major types portrayed by Hollywood. He had a drawl Southern accent, seldom spoke, and was always chewing tobacco. The last members of the group were Ali and his young apprentice, Yousif. Ali was mid-fifties and was the local guide from the Ministry of Electricity. He had supervised turbines and generators moving into Iraq many years previous and knew the route they needed to take to avoid any restrictions. Yousif was in his early twenties.

Major Joe explained the intention was to continue on the route through Ramadi, past Fallujah, and on into the Green Zone by nightfall. The following day we would complete the route from the Green Zone through the eastern side of Baghdad and onto Al Quds Power Station.

In order to discuss the various issues James and I got into the middle SUV with Joe, Davina, and Frank. I gave a radio to Jock, who was in the lead vehicle with Ali. If James needed to stop to check anything, then we could call him on the radio. Nigel and Ray brought up the rear in the armoured Land Cruiser. And off we went.

The remainder of the old road was uneventful, and soon we reached the outskirts of Ramadi. Joe had given us a quick intel brief of the hot spots, and this was definitely one of them. We would skirt around the northern suburbs until we reached the bridge over the Euphrates. At the bridge, James wanted to walk across. To my surprise, it was not the main bridge but the rickety old steel bridge we were to cross. There was a lot of local traffic using the bridge, and we were pretty vulnerable while out on foot. After a visual inspection, it was agreed that the bridge was to be load tested, which would be organised by Ali.

Instead of heading on along the route, we turned right just after the bridge and into a US Military camp. This was the headquarters of a unit from the 82nd Airborne. Joe suggested we touch base there and inform them of our intended transit through their TAOR (tactical area of responsibility). Sat in their comcen (command centre), Joe and I briefed their staff officers, and we were offered as much assistance as they could spare when we came through. I was particularly pleased, as I could see a need for some top cover on the main bridge as we crossed the steel bridge way down below.

As I walked through the comcen I noticed a cell for Sappers, this being the nickname for the Royal Engineers I had served in. After introducing myself and giving them a history lesson on where the term Sappers had come from, we went on to discuss the roadside IED problem. I am a former bomb disposal officer and was keen to glean any info they had and also to get as much intel about insurgency methods and activities as possible. They explained that the worst stretch of road was the main highway running to the north of Ramadi and Fallujah. The bad guys would come out at night and plant all the roadside bombs. Then the following morning, almost without fail a convoy would be hit. Their MO was to place a cluster of two or three IEDs on the side of the road and another cluster several hundred metres further on. They would then detonate both clusters to hit the front and rear of a convoy. They would then follow up with small-arms fire and then bug out (run away) before any follow-up force would arrive. The clusters were generally detonated by command wire out on the highway, but there had been instances of radio-controlled detonation in more built-up areas. The bad guys had learnt how to improvise with a remote control for garage doors. This was all good info.

I explained to the officers present that during the Troubles in Northern Ireland the Sappers had built a number of towers along the whole length of the border with Southern Ireland. They were referred to as the Romeo Towers and effectively gave continual observation along the border. I asked if they had considered building observation towers along the highway to prevent the bad guys the opportunity to come out at night.

Just as we were about finished, in walked the brigade commander, a one-star general. I was introduced and again gave a brief history lesson on Sappers. One of the staff officers then suggested I brief the general on the Romeo Towers. He appeared quite interested and directed his sappers to look into it.

By now it was late afternoon, and it was decided that we would stay in Camp Ramadi as we would not reach the Green Zone by nightfall. Dom had called, and they were safe at the border and had found someone to repair their tyre. We were shown to our accommodation for the night. It was a former palace of Uday, one of Saddam's sons. It had received some attention during the invasion and was barely standing. We slept in the basement. The US Military really knew how to live in style.

After another hearty breakfast we headed out from Camp Ramadi and up onto the highway heading East towards Baghdad. It was very quickly evident that the stretch of highway between Ramadi and Fallujah was a favourite hunting ground of the insurgency. Along the side of the road there were many scars and craters where roadside IEDs had been detonated and no doubt many lives had been lost. The Romeo Towers would greatly reduce this carnage.

We followed the highway for about 20 kilometres and then turned off to the left onto a track to avoid a low bridge. This track took us parallel to the highway until we reached a canal and another steel bridge. As James was out on foot, again assessing the bridge, we were also out keeping a watchful eye. It was early morning, and there were a fair amount of people out and about. Many on bicycles and small motorbikes. Then a car approached the bridge and pulled over to the side of the road. A male got out and raised the bonnet.

'Eyes open, guys,' I transmitted over the radio. 'Single male, car, bonnet open.'

The male was leaning on the front of the car, but his head was moving around and appeared to be watching and counting how many of us there were.

'We're being dicked,' declared Ray. A term used in Northern Ireland that meant you were being observed.

I could see Ray manoeuvring around so that he was behind the male but at a safe distance. Our intention was to keep him guessing where we were and how many of us there were. You either observe from a concealed position or you keep moving. Joe and Davina were sitting, chatting in the wagon. They appeared oblivious to the potential threat. After a couple of minutes the male closed the bonnet, without having done anything to the car. He got back in and drove back the same way he had come. What was his assessment, and where and what was he going to do next?

We were again in a vulnerable location under the main highway and wanted to get moving. I suggested to James we got going.

'Did you see the guy with the car?' he asked.

'Yep, and that's why I want to get going,' I replied.

Some people have a natural sense about what is going

on around them, and James appeared to be one. Others did not, and Joe and Davina fell into that category. Frank just had a scowl on his face. It wasn't easy to tell what he was thinking or aware of.

As we were mounting up, I passed Jock and said, 'I think we're being watched, so keep your eyes open.'

'Yeah, the guy with the car. Spotted him. Looked a bit shady,' said Jock. He was another one who was aware.

Our route then took us in a dead straight line for about 40 kilometres along a road known as RPG Alley. Davina had explained that she had lost two of her unit in an attack a few weeks previously. The road was flanked on both sides by small waterways, which effectively put you in a rat run with little room to manoeuvre. Due to the waterways and the relatively cool morning as we travelled along RPG Alley, there was a heavy mist hanging in the air. There was also quite a lot of vegetation. We picked up our speed. After about 10 kilometres I heard a distinctive click, then another two.

'Ray, you hear that?' I asked over the radio to the rear wagon.

'Negative, nothing heard,' replied Ray.

'High velocity' came Jock from the front wagon

'Roger that, let's keep going,' I said.

The click was from a high-velocity round passing. Probably from an AK-47. You don't often hear the thump of the weapon actually firing, but as the round passes, you hear a click as it passes over the speed of sound. The muzzle velocity of an AK-47 is around 710 metres per second, the speed of sound being 330 metres per second. So the round passes you or hits you before the sound of the weapon that fired it has reached you. If you do hear the thump of the weapon firing, firstly, it means you are still alive, and secondly, you can judge how far away it was fired. The effective range of an AK-47 is about 300 metres, and at the speed we were travelling we would be out of range within about ten seconds. This was why movement was our best defence.

'High velocity?' enquired James in a slightly stooped sitting position.

'Yeah, just a couple of rounds. Nothing to worry about,' I replied in a tone to keep things calm and to try and give the impression it was all in a day's work.

Davina and Joe started looking around with a bewildered look on their faces. I guessed they had missed it.

'AK from our right flank' was all Sergeant Major Frank said, without moving, except for his jaw chewing on his tobacco. He had clocked it. James was a little wide eyed and had a nervous grin on his face. We cracked on, and I was glad when we eventually turned southeast and in towards the outskirts of Baghdad.

To ram home how the potential of something nasty happening just when think you are emerging from a dangerous situation, I saw something that reminded me you have to be on your metal all the time. One of the snippets of intel I had picked up talking to some US troops was that they had come across IEDs hidden inside the bodies of dead dogs left on the road. As we had just turned off RPG Alley to the right side of the road was a dead dog. Running from its stomach area was what looked like a cable running off into the long grass. Perhaps a command wire to a firing point. But for whatever reason, thankfully no detonation. We were moving quite fast, so perhaps that was our saving grace. I informed Joe, who in turn called in the coordinates to the military.

As we approached the built-up area of Shu'la on the northwest of Baghdad, I could see it was a rundown area of the city. It was known as the meat market, and I soon saw why. There were row upon row of racks with goats and sheep hanging from their hind legs. I didn't realise at first that they were still alive until I saw a few wriggle. Then I saw a man draw up a large knife and slit a throat of one of them. After a few seconds of convulsions, the animal hung still as a stream of blood poured from its throat and flowed into a sea of blood and guts in the street. Even with the windows closed, the stench was over whelming, and I could literally see bow waves as our wagons travelled through the blood and guts which had formed between the curbs of the road. Locals were haggling over the price, and money was changing hands. I understood that this was obviously an age-old practice and the halal way of killing their food. I was sure the animal liberation parties would have a field day protesting here. I also smiled a little as I pictured Mrs Smith of suburbia tiptoeing through the carnage in her twin set and pearls to buy the family Sunday roast. Not quite the same as popping down to Tesco.

So far the route had been relatively easy to memorise, but we were now in a heavily built-up area. Amazingly, neither Davina nor Joe had maps, considering they had been in Baghdad for several months and belonged to allegedly the best-equipped army in the world. I began taking notes in my notebook but was also trying to keep an eye on any potential threats. Just off Highway 1, heading south towards the Green Zone, an overhead gantry caught James's attention and he wanted to measure it. Now we were out on foot at a busy intersection in Baghdad. Roof tops all around us and potentially hundreds of sniping locations. During phases between traffic lights James would go into the intersection and measure the height of the gantry. It was too low. Ali suggested that we could go up the ramp onto another road, cross the central barrier and then back down the other side to avoid the gantry. I don't know if James forgot where he was but he and Ali strode off to investigate this possibility. I quickly instructed Ray to stay with the wagon and for Nigel to come with me to provide some cover. We walked about

300 metres up the ramp onto the upper road, heavy traffic all around us. Up on the road we were level with the rooftops, and I could see people on the roofs. Some males with AKs, but this was becoming a familiar sight. When we started all this, I was not expecting to have to do foot patrols in Baghdad. But needs must, and James needed to do his job. We could see that the central barrier would have to be removed, but there was sufficient room for the trailers to swing around and back down. We returned to the vehicles. Jock was busy bollocking his team as they simply appeared to be standing around and not paying any attention to what was going on around them. I got the distinct impression they could not give a shit. It also went to reinforce discussions Steve and I had regarding not wanting to employ Iraqis. If these guys were allegedly former Saddam bodyguards, then the skill levels were woeful.

We continued on our route down towards the Green Zone, which was situated in Saddam's former palace right in the middle of Baghdad on the banks of the river Tigris. We did not follow the main Route 1 Highway but had to block around various route restrictions. We eventually came to the high concrete security perimeter of the Green Zone. We could not enter direct through one of the main gates. On arrival of the turbine and generator, the military would remove a section of the wall to allow access. All looked easy enough, and it was all down to coordination and timing.

We entered the Green Zone and headed for Saddam's presidential palace, which had been turned into transit accommodation. Inside what was once his prayer room, there were hundreds of bunk beds. There was a whole mixed bunch of contractors of all sorts of nationalities in there. We picked our beds and settled in.

The following morning we again set off at first light. The route took us out of the south of the Green Zone and immediately onto the Fourteenth of July Bridge over the

Tigris. Again the turbine and generator would not be going over this bridge but another rickety old steel bridge running alongside. We then headed left along the riverbank, and this time the roads were much more confined. There were many overhead electrical wires, and Ali was busy taking notes. As we made our way I could hear a series of explosions. Firstly off into the distance, but then they crept closer, the last being only a few streets away. The normal noises you associate with a city of traffic and voices were interspersed every now and again with machine gun fire, some way off in the distance and other very close. There was nothing in our immediate vicinity, so we cracked on. We made our way through mostly side roads towards the Army Canal Road, which we crossed perpendicular to and onto the western edge of Sadr City. This was a hot spot controlled by the Shia militant cleric Muqtada al-Sadr. Joe explained it was effectively a 'no go' area for the Army. Everyone was on full alert as we moved quickly along a service road running between the Army Canal Road and Sadr City.

We then turned north onto Route 2 Highway heading out of the city. As the landscape opened up and our fields of view expanded, I felt a little more in control. Probably not that I was—I just felt it. I was sure we could have been attacked just as easily out of town as inside. After about 20 kilometres we turned left off the highway, and a short distance later we arrived at the Al Quds Power Station. It was under construction, and on arrival I was introduced to Bob. He was a former US marine and was in charge of security. He explained that his security guard force was all recruited from the local villages. The previous day, approximately 300 metres of new fencing had been erected. This morning, when he completed his morning inspection, the whole 300 metres of new fencing had been stolen, right from under the noses of the so-called guards.

James went off to have a look at the foundations for

the turbine and generator, and I went for a brew with Bob. On seeing the FAL that Ray had, Bob became very excited and wanted to trade. He had used a British SLR many years before and thought it was a brilliant weapon. He explained that his site was mortared on a regular basis and he could often see the guys a few fields away but had nothing to engage them with from that distance. A good shot with an SLR could take someone out at 800 to 900 metres. Bob offered up three MP5s and a couple of AK-47s. More importantly, several thousand rounds of ammunition. As good as the FAL was, I agreed, and the deal was done.

We were due to head off back to the Green Zone when Jock approached me and asked for some contact details. He explained that he had not served with the British Military but had been in the French Foreign Legion for eleven years. I saw by the way he conducted himself that he knew what he was doing and stated I would be willing to take him on. After all, the best interview was to see the guy operating in the field. I certainly did not fancy being in his shoes, a lone Brit, with a bunch of Iraqis watching your back. I never saw or heard from him again. I hope he is still alive.

We separated from Ali, Jock, and their security team and made our way back into town towards the Green Zone. It was now late afternoon, and Joe said he would lead the way and our wagon at the rear. As we transited the city, we approached a short tunnel. Joe stopped on the down ramp blocking the road. We were flanked on each side by the wing walls about twenty feet down. Above the tunnel was a large roundabout and a large market place with lots of stalls. It was known as Thieves Market, as this was where most of the stolen property in Baghdad was sold.

'They often throw IEDs off the bridge onto our Humvees, so I want to let the tunnel clear so we have a clear run through,' explained Joe. By now we were already out of our wagon, and there was a large backlog of vehicles behind our roadblock. Understandably, they were frustrated and started honking their horns, which in turn was drawing a lot of attention to our situation. I got James to crouch down besides the wagon. I did not want him inside a vehicle if we got attacked. I could not believe what Joe had done. We were effectively trapped like rats in a barrel, in full view of many, many people above us. To add to it, Joe, Frank, and Davina were in full US Military uniform and each only armed with a pistol. I looked down into the tunnel and could see the tail end of the traffic slowly inching forward. In the distance I could again hear small arms fire. Far enough away so as not to be anything to do with us, but I was expecting any second that either we would be shot at or an IED would explode. Out of all the time I spent in Iraq, this was the most scared I was. There were three military and three civilian security guys, surrounded by several hundred Iraqis. And we were trapped. I shot a glance at Ray and Nigel and could see they were equally nervous. Ray frowned and mouthed to me, 'What the fuck is going on?'

'Keep moving. Bob, and weave,' I said to them both. If anyone was lining up a shot, I wanted to at least make it difficult for them.

I was not sure what order things happened next. Whether the crown ran away from one side of the wall because there was someone possibly coming or Nigel bearing his weapon in their direction. Or Nigel bore his weapon because they ran away, expecting some bad guys with guns to appear. Whatever, you could have cut the tension with a knife. I looked at Davina and could see she had gone pale. I think even Joe suddenly realised our situation and gave a wave to get going. We needed no second invitation, and we mounted our wagon, and we got going. By the time we reached the far end of the tunnel, the up ramp was still congested. Thankfully, after a minute or two, it cleared, and we picked up speed. We got back to the

Green Zone a short time later. But I could not help but wonder why Joe had brought us that route when there had been so many attacks there and it was always congested.

The route survey completed the following day, we drove James back to the Jordanian border. We met up with Dom and his crew and gave them another repaired tyre we had managed to get fixed. There were a number of points on the route where some civil works were needed, which would take some time to arrange and complete. It was agreed that James would liaise with Osama from Khuene + Nagel and would give us three days' notice to deploy with the full security team.

We headed back to BIAP to stay for the night before returning to Kuwait. That night, I lay on my cot thinking this was not how I had intended to celebrate my fortieth birthday.

The trip back south from Baghdad to the Kuwait border was uneventful. No problems refuelling and a clear run all the way. We reached the border, and just short, I gave the word over the radio to stash the weapons. We hid them under the seats, and the military gave a cursory look inside as we cleared through the search lanes.

FINAL PREP

Back at the villa I updated Steve and the ops room staff on our trip. I had taken some video footage of some points on the route and gave a general briefing to all the guys. We were still one guy short, and we still did not have enough weapons for the whole team. I envisaged we would have about three or four days before we get the call up. I gave a set of orders to the guys and divided them into their vehicles and nominated vehicle commanders.

I gave the vehicle call signs and deployed them as follows:

Lima – This was to be the left forward vehicle and would have Dom as vehicle commander and then Kerry Jones, Rich Stanley, and John Fisher as crew. Their role was to provide left forward recce and to suss out any potential attack locations off to the left-hand side of the road.

Romeo – This was the right forward recce and would have Ray as vehicle commander and then Gareth Evans, Julian Moses, and Rob Burns as crew. Their role the same as Lima, but off to the right.

Sierra – This was to be the sweep vehicle and would travel pretty much in line with the forward recce and check the road, culverts, and bridges for IEDs. It would travel a tactical bound in front of the main convoy. This meant just far enough forward that if anything happened, the convoy was separate, but also close enough that we could get back quickly. As this was the best place to dictate deployment on the move, this is where I located myself. In addition, I was EOD (explosive ordnance disposal) trained and also search trained. Also in the vehicle was Sammy Dunn, another former Sapper with search training. Nigel would act as my sergeant major, and then to provide some infantry cover,

Matt Jones, a former platoon sergeant from the RRW.

Foxtrot – The vehicle would travel immediately in front of the convoy and provide front protection. The vehicle commander was Martin Callaghan. He was a former para and also ex-RUC Special Branch. He was an older guy, and I thought the maturity and experience would be useful there. His crew was Malcolm Miller, Marc Collins, and Richard Platt.

Bravo – This would be the backstop vehicle and would provide rear protection to the convoy. This was commanded by Andy Christie, or Chalky, as he was known. His crew was Matt Williams, Andy Palfreman, and Mark Nuth

The guys had been training, but now they worked in their vehicle teams. They practiced wheel changing and casualty evacuation. Within the group, there were enough instructors in the various disciplines; weapon, medical, and signals training took place.

A few days later I took two vehicles, and we took a trip up over the border into Iraq. Just up on Route Tamper, we came across an Iraqi police checkpoint. Previously we had not stopped at any of these, as they really did not have any jurisdiction then and certainly not the confidence to stop what looked like a bunch of Western private security contractors. However, this time I wanted to stop. I found one that spoke English and asked him to take me to his boss. He took me to his captain, and I asked the same. He took me to his colonel, and he in turn took me to a guy who he said was a local sheik. This was at a villa on the outskirts of Basra. The sheik did not speak English, but the colonel did, and through him we eventually danced around the issue that I wanted to buy weapons. I know you would not normally ask the local police to buy illegal weapons. But this was Iraq, and the Yankee dollar talked.

We sat crossed-legged in the grounds of the sheik's

villa, drinking far too much tea and making small talk. After about two hours, some guys came in with some AKs. Unbelievably, the colonel loosed off half a mag at a palm tree in the corner. He belly laughed and handed me the weapon. I followed suit and emptied the mag. Chalky looked over a few of the other AKs, and they were in good condition. There were also a few RPKs, which were the larger machine gun variant in the Kalashnikov series. It was magazine fed and would be useful.

Stuffed into the pockets of my khaki cargo trousers, I had bundles of US dollars. For the weapons and ammunition, we agreed on a price, and I handed over just over $24,000. I had a further $11,000 on me, and although there was the potential for us all to get turned over and robbed by these guys, sometimes you have to make a judgement call and go with your gut instinct. We were paying them a good price for their guns, and I had stated we would need more. We came away with a further ten AK-47s and five RPKs. And again, just as important, several thousand rounds of ammunition.

We were to visit the good colonel many times again, and he was to become a good friend. Again, for obvious reasons, his name is omitted for his own safety.

We stowed the weapons and ammunition into the vehicles, hiding them under the rear seats of the Nissan Patrols. After a short drive back to the border, we approached the checkpoint manned by the Kuwaiti Army. We pulled over and stepped out of the vehicles, leaving all doors open, inviting them to search the vehicle. My heart was pounding underneath my body armour. We had enough weapons and ammo to start a small war, and I guess the Kuwaitis would not take too kindly to a bunch of Brits smuggling this lot over the border. After a cursory glance into the rear of the vehicle, we were waved on. Just over 500 metres further on was a sterner test. The US Military checkpoint. They had lanes set up for searching of all vehicles. I guess this was why the Kuwaitis did not complete any form of search, rather to rely on the US Military to pick up anything.

Again we stepped out of the vehicles, leaving all doors open. A few pleasantries were exchanged with the troops. I was asked where our security details were. I explained they had left us at the border and had returned to their base in Basrah. It appeared to have washed. A halfhearted search was made of the rear compartment, and a glance into the crew compartments was made. After only about thirty seconds, we were waved on.

We drove on into Kuwait and headed back to the villa, breathing a big sigh of relief. We were now fully equipped for the task at hand, except for one guy short and no decent maps. But hey, not bad for just over ten days of preparation.

THE CONVOY

Eight days passed, and we had not been called forward. The guys were getting bored, but at least we were on standby rates, and the bills were being covered. Training had been ongoing, but there was only so much we could do that did not involve weapons. Then we got the call to deploy.

After a quick set of confirmatory orders, the rest of the day was spent loading the vehicles in preparation for an early departure from the villa to reach the border to cross at first light.

At 0400 hrs the armoury opened, and an orderly queue formed as weapons and ammo were handed out by Shep. The smell of gun oil and full-fried breakfast filled the basement of the villa. There was a buzz of excitement, and I felt the butterflies in my stomach as a slight surge of adrenaline kicked in, thinking about what we were about to embark on. One by one all five vehicles backed up against the ops room, just above the steps that led up from the basement. The guys had been repeatedly briefed that all weapons were to be loaded to vehicles, as much as possible out of sight of neighbouring villas, for obvious reasons. By 0430 hrs all vehicles were lined up and ready to go.

Steve staggered out from his bedroom in shorts and T-shirt to see us off. Shep did his rounds, and I could see him muttering to all the guys and shaking their hands. Shep was the oldest there, and it was like he was seeing his children off to school. He came to me last and, again with a sombre face, gave me a firm handshake, and in unison we both said, 'Stay low, move fast, trust no one.' Shep smiled, turned, and walked inside.

After a quick radio check we pulled out the rear gates

of the villa and onto the Fifth Ring Road. There was very little traffic about, and we made good progress, reaching the border in just over an hour. I went to the US Military office and booked out a trip ticket. When I returned, the guys had suited up with body armour, and we were ready to cross.

Just after 0530 hrs the sun was up, and the border point was open. We slowly moved forward, handed over the trip ticket to the marine, and we headed the kilometre towards the Iraqi side of the border. We had got in front of all the truck convoys which had been lined up in the staging area, and I made a mental note that if we were to pick up guarding truck convoys, we could expect delays in just getting over the border. At present the US Military were still providing convoy protection. We crossed the border into Iraq, and after about 100 metres there was a staging area off to the side of the road. Over the radio I instructed all to pull over, tool up, and get ready to roll in two minutes. We pulled in, and just out of sight of the checkpoint we all took our weapons and magazines out from their hiding places and loaded. Without too much delay we were off.

As we went through the border village of Safwan, the kids were again out early, patting their stomachs, begging for food. I quickly reminded all over the radio not to throw any food or drink. We had heard that a soldier in a US Military convoy had thrown some food rations out, and a small child who had run forward to pick it up had been struck by the following vehicle and killed. We turned left onto route Tamper and headed north towards Baghdad. We stopped briefly at Camps Cedar and Scannia and refuelled at both. The journey passed without incident, and by late afternoon we had reached BIAP. We booked into the tented accommodation at the staging area and then headed for the DEFAC. As the guys went in to eat, I made a call to the ops room to give an update over the sat phone. I had a good night's sleep, broken only once by the sound of a few distant mortars.

At daft o'clock in the morning we were all up again and heading for yet more stodge at the DEFAC. Just as first light appeared, we were all lined up near the exit gate, ready for the 553 kilometre trip west to the Jordanian border. Davina, Major Joe, and Frank joined us. After about 50 kilometres we passed north of Fallujah and Ramadi. Again the highway was scattered with burnt-out vehicles and bomb craters on the side of the road. Looked like the insurgents were still busy planting their overnight IEDs. We travelled at a steady 140 kilometres per hour with 50 metre spacing, keeping to the centre lane as much possible. As we approached overpasses the guys began to adopt the habit of going from lane to lane to keep any would-be detonators guessing as to which lane we would be in as we passed them. I made regular checks on the fuel levels, and all was going well. We reached the US Military camp at the border by early afternoon. I was pleased that we were now at the border, fully ready for the convoy to cross over the border the following day. We were still one man short of the twenty guys we were supposed to have, but I was hoping that would be resolved shortly. I had a mobile signal and called James to let him know we had arrived.

First light was about 0530 hrs, and the convoy was already rumbling towards the border crossing point. Walking in front with the broadest smile on his face was James. Behind him was his train set. Two specialist hydraulic trailers, each with ninety-six tyres and being pulled by Scammell tractors. The tractors were special low-ratio geared and heavily ballasted to be able to pull the 250 ton loads. The tractors were old, even older than me, but as James explained, 'Nothing pulls like a Scammell.' Behind the two trailers were a spare tractor, a support container on a truck, and two pieces of plants to assist with any unexpected civil works needed. In all, the convoy was over 700 metres long, and all had to be protected.

'Good morning,' boomed James in a best of British accent.

'Well, good morning to you too, my dear chap. And how are you this fine sunny morning? Is your hat at a jaunty angle, and is there a skip in your step?' I replied in what was becoming a Monty Pythonesque routine between James and me.

'My hat is indeed at a jaunty angle, and my step has a skip in it. Ready for the off and ready for whatever Johnny Foreigner has to throw at us. Let us sally forth,' retorted James.

Body armour and helmets were issued to the ALE crew. James, Davina, and me had a quick briefing together, and we were ready to roll. Romeo and Lima headed off to the right and left forward flanks, respectively, and Sierra took point on the road. Foxtrot was positioned about 100 metres further back, just in front of the convoy, and Bravo settled in just behind the convoy. Bravo was the most heavily armed, as it was potentially the most vulnerable at the rear.

A small plume of smoke and a roar from the tractors and the convoy slowly picked up speed to its maximum of 10 kilometres per hour. I again thought what an excellent target practice this would all be for the bad guys.

Romeo and Lima sped ahead several hundred metres and began fanning out either side of the road looking for potential firing positions, not only for small arms but also command wire IEDs. The land either side of the road was wide open desert with mostly hard stony ground, which was ideal for the 4×4s to travel. At first they were heading too far, and often we lost sight of them. But after an hour or two the guys settled into a reasonable distance from the axis we were travelling.

I was in Sierra, which travelled a few hundred metres ahead of the convoy. As well as command and control, my team was also responsible for checking all culverts and bridges for potential IEDs. There would be no time for a full controlled search, only a quick visual search. Within the first couple of kilometres it became quickly apparent that while it looked like a wide open desert, there were culverts every few hundred metres. Sammy and I were both search trained, and I was also an ex-EOD officer. It was our job to do the visual checks. Nigel and Matt took turns in driving and general lookout. At each culvert we would stop the vehicle short. Sammy and I would then jog forward, down the embankment, and adopt the press-up position. Mostly we could see each other through opposite ends of the culverts, and they were clear. Some had sand blown in and were totally blocked. Potentially a good hiding place for an IED. But again we did not have time to fully check because even though the convoy was moving slowly, it would soon catch us up. So we also relied on further visual checks of the surrounding area for signs of disturbance, footprints, buried wires, or anything else that just looked out of place.

We had scraped ice of our windscreen first thing in the morning, and for the first few hours we were wearing fleeces under our body armour. By about 10:00 am it had warmed sufficiently to reduce down to a T-shirt. As the day progressed and we slowly trundled across the western Iraqi desert, Sammy and I were certainly putting in the work. We saw very little other traffic as we were on the old road running parallel to the main highway. Towards late afternoon I tasked Romeo and Lima to shoot forward about five klicks (kilometres) to locate a suitable overnight stop. By about 4:00 pm we had travelled a total distance of just over 80 kilometres, and Sammy and I had searched about 100 culverts. It was steady physical work, and although I was not totally knackered, I was looking forward to a lie-down and a rest.

We had found an old derelict building off to the right

of the road with a large hard standing big enough to pull the convoy onto. I quickly circled the location on foot and positioned each team for its night's stay. I asked James to tell his guys to keep any lights to an absolute minimum during darkness. No point in drawing attention to ourselves. Nigel was doing his sergeant major bit and getting around the guys, checking on them and drawing up a stag roster for the night's roaming guard.

I called into the ops room over the sat phone to give an update. I was informed by Chris that our twentieth man had been secured and he was on a flight to Amman, Jordan, and that he would be at the border by about midnight. So far we had managed to keep the fact we only had nineteen men from Davina. All I had to do now was to sneak out and pick our man up from the border. It got dark about 6:00 pm, and with very little else to do, most settled down for the night. I guessed that as we had travelled 80 kilometres, we could be back at the border within forty-five minutes. I planned to leave at 11:00 pm, by which time I was hoping Davina would be fast asleep and none the wiser.

I was conscious that it was not sound planning for one vehicle to travel on its own, especially at night. But bearing in mind our remoteness, I decided to take the risk. Just before 11:00 pm my team climbed into Sierra. Sammy let off the handbrake, and we rolled silently away off down a slope away from the convoy. We had positioned the vehicles so we could do this without any fuss. Several hundred metres away Sammy started the engine, and off we sped towards the border.

The guy we were to pick up was a Scouser called Rob, and I had interviewed him a few months ago. He had served with the King's Regiment (Infantry) and later transferred to the paras. I was not overly impressed with him and found him a little strange. But as the guys in the ops room had been chasing around the telephone list I had left, Rob knocked on the door of the villa in Kuwait and asked if there was any work going. Apparently, he had already been working in Iraq and had just returned into Kuwait, having completed a short contract. Perhaps a stroke of luck for us.

A little after midnight I called the mobile number given, and Rob answered. He was just clearing immigration, and shortly afterwards, I could see him walking across no man's land towards the border exit gate. Wearing jeans and a large thick cream-coloured cardigan, I could not say he looked the part.

'All right, guys, how you doing?' Rob said in a grating Scouser accent, but with a beaming smile.

I caught a look at Sammy as he shot a glance at Matt and rolled his eyes. One thing I learnt from my time in the Army was how quickly soldiers could sum someone up. But I guess Rob was a new guy to the team and this was to be expected. Rob was given a set of body armour and a weapon. Nigel gave a quick briefing to Rob as we made our way back to the convoy location. As we approached, the sentries had been briefed to expect us around 1:00 am. After giving the agreed signal of three quick flashes we returned to our slot in the perimeter and bedded down for the night. As I climbed into my maggot (sleeping bag), I thought of the village of Ar Rutbah we would come across tomorrow. I slept well.

The following morning there was some cloud in the sky, and the temperature was a little warmer. No ice on the windscreens today. After a quick bite to eat we settled into our convoy positions. James approached me and asked if he could have a radio in case he needed to contact me.

'Sure,' I said. 'You can be Juliet.'

James looked at me with a slightly quizzical look. 'You know, Juliet, for J. J for James.' I explained and turned and walked away. As I did so, I pressed the button on my radio. 'Hello, Juliet, this is Sierra. Radio check, over.'

In a very slow and sarcastic tone, James replied, 'Hello, Sierra, this is Ju-li-et. Shove it up your arse, OUT.' I glanced back to see James laughing. He is a good egg, I thought.

After a couple of hours and many culverts later, we approached the outskirts of Ar Rutbah. Matt and Sammy had found the name of the village amusing and kept putting on a surprised look and saying, 'Ahh, Rutbah!' as if startled by suddenly seeing it. There had been some reports of insurgency activity in the vicinity, and as we had found on our recce, we did not have to go right through the centre of the town. We had discussed how we would dismount and provide a walking cordon through such a situation. I adopted point in the centre of the road. Each vehicle had a driver with the doors left open and slowly crept forward. Davina approached me and asked why we were out on foot. I explained that if the vehicle is moving in anything less than walking pace, then we dismounted, as we were less of a target if dispersed. Many of the guys had Northern Ireland experience, and I could quickly see the guys adopting the non-aggressive patrol approach. This meant they cradled their weapons rather than the more aggressive stance of the butt of the weapon at the shoulder. Many of the local inhabitants began to appear along the roadside. My eyes were scanning for signs of weapons or any unusual activity. But most just stood and stared at us.

'Hearts and minds,' I said over the radio and began to smile and greet the odd person. Many of the guys followed. We wanted to give the impression we were not a threat to them and just wanted to be on our way without any fuss. Nigel was off to my right about 15 metres away and on the sidewalk. Up ahead of him I could see something that would attract his attention. As he approached, he noticed and gave a big thumbs up. In front of him stood a young lad about 10 years old, wearing an Arsenal football top. Nigel was an avid

Arsenal fan, and with his thumb up and a big beaming smile, the young lad followed suit and also put his thumb up and smiled.

'Arsenal, yeah,' Nigel said to the lad. A few adults in the close proximity smiled, and I could feel the tension relax a little.

Then one of the older men asked, 'British?'

Nigel again stuck up his thumb, smiled, and replied, 'Yeah, British.'

The man smiled back then pointed towards me, frowning, and asked, 'American?'

Nigel replied, 'No, British,' and again put up his thumb and said, 'Yeah.' The young lad mimicked Nigel and shouted, 'British, yeah,' holding up his thumb.

Nigel then pulled a frown and, with his thumb pointing down, replied, 'American, boo.'

The old man laughed and copied 'American, boo,' with his thumb pointing down. Within seconds Nigel had the small crowd chanting 'British, yeah. American, boo', with alternating thumbs up and down. Many were smiling and laughing, and while I was conscious we did not need any distraction, this side show was a distraction for the locals as the convoy rumbled passed, turned left, and headed out of the town.

Nigel had become surrounded by kids and was like the Pied Piper of Hamelin. He was beginning to drop back as the convoy steadily pushed on out of town. I quickly signalled Sammy to swing our vehicle off the road and hang back.

'Sorry, kids, we've got to go,' I shouted with a big theatrical wave and smile and nodded to Nigel to get to the vehicle. By now the rear of the convoy was about 600 metres away and we were becoming detached. Nigel and I both stepped onto the side sills of the vehicle, and Sammy eased away as we both gave big waves to the kids.

'Well, at least they appeared to like us,' Nigel said.

Sierra resumed its place at point on the road, and we were back to culverts again.

As we moved slowly eastwards, progress was slow, and we settled into a routine. We ate on the hoof with frequent snacks from the MREs. These were the US Military rations called Meals Ready to Eat or, as some called them, Meals Rejected by Ethiopians. They were not all that bad and were ideal for continual snacking, as we were burning a lot of calories.

Most of the road was hard-top tarmac, but some parts were gatched track, which threw up a lot of dust. The crews of the trailers were mostly Indians, and sat on a small seat on the back of the trailer was a steersman. His job was to keep the hydraulic trailer level and compensate for cambers and slopes. One of the steersman was called Shukla, and he had been with ALE for many years. It was obvious he was the supervisor, as he was always barking orders to the crews. In the back of my wagon, I had a Kevlar helmet with a bulletproof visor. It was intended for wearing while prodding for mines, but I thought would be ideal for the steersmen to protect their faces from all the stones being thrown up by the trailer. I gave one to the steersman. Shukla had a big smile on his face, and I think he quite liked being different from the other guys.

Midafternoon, and as I ran down a small embankment to the right of the road to check yet another set of culverts, I saw three artillery shells just sitting about 10 metres off the side of the road. I instinctively dropped to the floor. But then I could see there were no wires attached. I approached and saw that the shells had been hollowed out. No danger to us, so I continued the search of the culverts. Just as I reached the end of a set of about six culverts, I then saw what appeared to be the tail section of a missile. It was heavily corroded, and I guessed it was a remnant of

Operation Desert Storm back in 1991. Again, no danger to us.

Over the next four days, we travelled over the open desert heading towards the next built-up area of Ramadi. At this time, it was the main insurgent stronghold along with its neighbouring town of Fallujah. We were due to link up with the US Military about 10 kilometres west of Ramadi. They were to provide an outer cordon and SFI the inner cordon to move around the northern outskirts of Ramadi and Fallujah. I was expecting at least a company of infantry (approximately two hundred men). But as we approached the RV, I could see only two Humvees. A total of six soldiers. Davina introduced herself, and after an exchange of salutes, she sprang into life, barking orders at her uniformed colleagues. Until now she had been very quiet, but I guess now she had to make a mark.

We settled the convoy into a rest area and discussed how we would move over the next two days past probably two of the most hostile towns in the world. My main concern was the Ramadi Bridge, as it was a real choke point for us. I explained to the sergeant that the convoy only moved a maximum of 10 kilometres per hour. He appeared genuinely surprised, and despite pointing out the fact we had discussed this with his HQ on the recce, it was obvious he had simply been briefed to escort a couple of vehicles though their area and expected they would travel at normal speed.

Just then John Fisher came to see me and explained he had a roaring toothache. I looked at him, and he was nearly in tears. The right side of his face was swollen, and I could tell he was in immense pain. I asked the sergeant if there was a medical centre at his base, to which he confirmed there was.

I took Davina aside and suggested that we go into the base and seek dental treatment for John. I then firmly suggested that while we did that, she and I went to the HQ and establish if there was to be any further military assistance for the move over the Ramadi Bridge.

'I guess that would be a sensible thing to do,' Frank added in a knowing way.

I detailed off two vehicles to prepare to head into Ramadi. After getting a brief and directions from the sergeant, I further briefed the guys that it was not a welcoming place and that we would be travelling at speed. It was late afternoon, and we had about two hours of daylight left. I did not expect to get in and back out before darkness fell. But I was happier heading into town in daylight.

The first few klicks were open road, and we progressed quickly. We encountered more and more traffic as we approached the outskirts of the town. The base was in the centre, and with only about a klick to go the traffic was gridlocked over a bridge. I looked at the map and saw an alternative route. Thankfully, there was less traffic, but still quite heavy. As we approached the base and the series of chicanes, I could see that the entrance to the camp was heavily guarded, complete with M1 main battle tank and numerous heavy machine gun posts. To avoid any blue on blue, I slowed the vehicle down and held out a Union Jack. The sentry indicated for me to approach on foot. I got out of the vehicle and clearly showed my arms were out to my sides. I left my MP5 on the seat of the car and only had a pistol in a holster strapped to my right leg. As I approached and the sentry could clearly see I was a Westerner, he lowered his weapon. It was obviously a heavily defended camp in the middle of one of the worst towns, and I really did fear some trigger-happy, nervous young GI letting loose with a few rounds in my direction. Not to mention we were still on the outside and at our most vulnerable to attack from our rear. I could only imagine what would happen if some bad guys opened up on us from the rear. The military would probably mistake the shooting coming from us, and we would get it from both sides.

Without incident we entered that camp and followed directions to the dental centre. John went in, and the other guys headed off to the DEFAC, never missing an opportunity for a good scoff. Davina and I went over to the HQ. About two weeks previously I had been welcomed into the HQ. I don't know what had happened in the meantime, but I was turned away at the door. Davina went in to negotiate more troops. I headed back over to the dental centre.

On enquiring after John I was shown through a door. As I went into what turned out to be the operating theatre, I could see John reclined back in a chair. Towering over him was a huge black female nurse. I wasn't sure if she was pinning him down or about to mount him. I have never seen a grown man more frightened in my life. After picking myself off the floor from laughing, I asked what was happening. The nurse explained the doctor would be in soon to treat John and pointed to a seat. I took a big step backwards and avoided being pinned in any chair by this immense woman. She would be capable of breaking a man's back!

I picked up a copy of Stars and Stripes, a military magazine, and began reading an article. I was vaguely aware of the doctor coming into the room, and after about thirty seconds I heard him say, 'OK, that's it.' I heard a clink as John's tooth was dropped into a bowl. The doc had pulled the tooth, and John sat in his chair, looking pale and as if he had been through ten rounds with Mike Tyson. John was handed some antibiotics and sent on his way. I assisted him as he gingerly walked out. The big black nurse smiled and wiggled her fingers as a wave bye bye.

'I think you pulled there, mate,' I said to John as we headed out.

'Get me back out there, where it's safer,' replied John. I laughed.

We headed over to the DEFAC, and I grabbed some stodge while John ate some ice cream. The rest of the guys were stuffed and enjoying a bit of banter with the soldiers. I couldn't help but notice how young they all looked. Or was I just getting old?

We headed back out to the vehicles to wait for Davina. As we chatted I could hear the odd muffled explosion off into the distance as well as the odd burst of machine gun fire. Some not so far off.

Davina eventually came out, and with a big beaming smile on her face, I knew it was good news.

'OK, we will get as much support as they can spare for the crossing of the bridge tomorrow morning and some extra Humvees for the remainder of the route north of Fallujah,' she said. Not conclusive or definite, I thought, but I understood the operational pressures the military would be under.

'I'm going to grab a quick shower,' stated Davina as she headed off with several offers from the guys to scrub her back. We headed back to the DEFAC for a coffee. After all, we had only been in the field for seven days, and we had showers planned for the Green Zone in a couple of days' time.

About twenty minutes later Davina returned with wet hair and smelling like a woman should.

'Watch you don't drive the guys wild,' I teased. Davina blushed.

We mounted up and headed out of the base. It was dark, and not many streetlights were working. Thankfully, the roads were a lot quieter, and we soon picked up speed. I was smiling to myself at the sight of John cowering under the nurse. Suddenly, to our right and at close range, a short burst of machine gun fire. I peered out into the darkness but could not see anything. Over the roar of the engine, as we sped away, I asked the other vehicles if they were OK. All was good and another little incident chalked down to some good luck.

We arrived back at the convoy base about 10:00 pm and found that there were only the two Humvees as additional protection. The guys settled back in, and I crawled into my maggot. After what only seemed like a few minutes' sleep, I was awoken by Rob. He was deep breathing, and I could see his pupils were wide. He started to explain that while he was on roving guard he had seen four men approaching with weapons. He stated he had challenged them, and they ran off. Due to our location, I assessed that we would not be on anyone's foot passage to anywhere. Therefore, could only assume they were here to cause us harm. I got up and spoke with some of the other guys, and no one else had seen or heard anything. Then Rob changed his story several times, and I began to think he was making this up. I checked my watch, and it was 2:00 am. I decided to go and speak to the military, as they should have good night vision and would have seen them. In any case, they needed to be aware of the potential threat.

As I approached the Humvee I was conscious that we were effectively out in the desert and did not want to startle them. But of course they would have seen me approaching as they would have been awake and alert? I peered through the side window and could see all three occupants were fast asleep. I decided that rather than wake them and risk one of them loosing off their weapon, I quietly turned and walked back to the inner cordon. I guess we were not going to rely on our cousins from over the pond too much. The rest of the night passed without incident, but I made a note to self to keep an eye on Rob.

Early the next day I gathered the vehicle commanders in, and we talked through the move over the bridge and up onto the main highway. We then had about 20 kilometres to travel before turning off left onto a track to cross another bridge over a canal. The intention was to complete this all within the day so that we would be clear of Ramadi and Fallujah in one go. There were some sombre-looking faces. So far, we had navigated open desert, where our fields of observation were good. From now on it was more urban and lots of potential for ambush, IEDs, and snipers.

Most guys I had spoken to were most worried about roadside IEDs. My view was that if one went off right next to you, then you would not know much about it. Most agreed that an ambush with small-arms fire was more down to a fifty-fifty fire fight, and at least you had a chance of getting them before they got you. My biggest concern was a sniper. Almost impossible to detect and counter in an urban setting. But most of all, a sniper gave you no opportunity to at least have a fight. Not that I wanted to be killed, but if I were to be killed, I would want to have at least had the slightest chance to fight back before I bought it.

We set off, and after about ten klicks we reached the Ramadi Bridge going over the Euphrates. It was an old steel bridge set down to the side of the main highway bridge. The Ministry had carried out a very scientific method for load testing the bridge. They had driven a number of trucks onto the bridge with concrete blocks weighing a total of three hundred tons. The bridge had not collapsed, so it was safe. I just hoped it had not weakened it and by the next heavy load it would collapse.

To my surprise and delight, as we approached I would see US Military all over the place. Above on the highway bridge were a couple of Humvees and several more positioned at either end of the bridge. It was a good turnout. If anyone were to have a pop, then they would do well to do so and get away again.

I had briefed for Romeo, Lima, and Sierra to cross the bridge first and secure the far bank. With the amount of troops about, it was fairly superfluous, but I was keener to get across and off the bridge before the first heavy trailer got on. We dismounted and spread out. I looked back to see James striding down the centre of the bridge with the first tractor and trailer slowly inching forward behind him. He was extremely vulnerable not only from sniper fire but also from the bridge collapsing. I felt a bit guilty leaving him out there, so I also headed onto the bridge. Not that I would be able to stop much, but at least if someone were lining up a shot and I kept moving around him, it may put off a would-be sniper.

'Good morning, turned out nice again,' I shouted, as I was still some distance away from James.

'Yes, lovely day for a stroll down by the river, don't you think?' replied James with a broad smile on his face.

'Hope it holds,' I said.

'No worries,' James replied as he stamped his foot down with a cringing look on his face. Then laughed out loud.

I walked along with James, continually circling him. I tried not to make it too obvious. There was lots of creaking and groaning coming from the bridge, but slowly the first trailer cleared and headed off towards the highway. The second trailer then edged onto the bridge, and thankfully, without incident, the crossing of the Ramadi Bridge was completed.

The convoy headed up onto the highway, which was raised about 10 metres above the surrounding land. It was heavily built up on either side, with buildings only about 100 metres either side of the road. The traffic was fairly light, as there were still not too many cars available in Iraq. It was already early afternoon, and I was concerned we would not clear the northern edge of Fallujah before darkness fell. As we settled into a steady 10 kilometres per hour, the checking of culverts became a rushed affair as they were numerous and the embankments were much bigger. After about half an hour I looked back and saw that all the military support we had was peeling off. On checking with Davina, I was told that we were crossing their boundary of responsibility and would hand us over to another unit. We continued on. Civilian traffic passed on the outside lane and was closely watched by our guys. After about an hour and as darkness approached we were joined by two Humvees, who informed us they were our escorts. We discussed that we would not make it off the highway before darkness. Romeo and Lima went ahead and reported a large lay-by where we could stop overnight. Thankfully, the highway had begun to swing away from the town, and the nearest buildings were now at least 600 metres away. With night sights, we would have reasonably good fields of view and would see anything approaching. My only concerns were that some civilian traffic was still travelling the highway after dark, and there was also an overbridge about 200 metres to our rear which restricted our view.

As we settled in, I overheard Davina giving orders to the few military guys present to position them on the highway. The sergeant was politely explaining that their orders were to return to the camp to refuel and return in the morning. I guess we were to be on our own tonight.

I had given orders that there were to be no lights at all. We were sat on a raised road and could be seen for miles around. As I wandered around, chatting to the guys, I had to ask James to get his guys to conceal any lights they needed to use. It was a little difficult to explain the importance of light discipline to a bunch of Indian guys. I then came across about six of our guys standing, looking out into the desert, all holding night sights. Perhaps they had seen some movement out there, I thought.

'See something?' I asked Dom.

'Davina's taking a dump,' he replied without lowering his night sight.

'Thank God I've already eaten,' I said as I left them to it.

I chatted with James for about half an hour and then headed for my tent. I was just about to pull back the flaps when a distinctive clicking passed overhead, followed by the sound of gunfire off to our rear. I estimated about 300 metres away. I then heard the roar of a car engine, and it was heading towards us. There were shouts of 'Stand to' from some of the guys, and I could hear weapons being cocked. The headlights of the approaching car were swerving all over the road. But then it straightened up and was accelerating hard.

'Hold your fire!' I could hear Chalky shouting.

It quickly became apparent the car was in the outside lane and was going to pass by. We had been told there were many carjacking at night, and I assumed this guy had just got away. I made my way towards the rear of the area we were in. Lying flat under a crash barrier was Stan. He was looking through a set of NVGs (night vision goggles).

Very quietly and calmly he reported, 'Two hundred metres, two males, both armed with AKs on the hard shoulder, walking this way.'

'I think it was an attempted carjacking,' said Chalky as he quietly crouched down beside me.

'Yeah, agreed. Get around and check if anyone was hit,' I replied.

'Roger that,' said Chalky and disappeared.

'Stan, keep an eye on them,' I said and moved back about 5 metres. 'Dom, take one guy and position yourself about 20 metres to the right,' I said, indicating with my arm. 'On my command, light them up with your torches. Any aggressive movement from them, and we'll take them out from over here.' There was a lot of activity but very little noise as Dom positioned himself. I grabbed Sammy and Matt and positioned them with me under the crash barrier next to

Stan. He still had an eyeball on them.

'One hundred metres,' whispered Stan.

It was pitch black, and I was confident these two guys had not seen or heard anything of us. I was banking on them being taken totally by surprise and would just throw down their weapons. I decided to spring the surprise when they were about 40 metres away.

'Eighty metres,' whispered Stan.

What these guys were doing was wrong. Stealing cars was a crime, but these were not insurgents. I felt like judge, jury, and executioner.

'Fifty metres,' whispered Stan.

In the dark I could just make out two figures approaching.

'Forty metres,' whispered Stan. I hesitated for a split second, probably more to clear my throat, which was dry.

'They've stopped,' whispered Stan.

I was about to give the order when Stan whispered, 'They're turning around and heading back.'

Stan gave a running commentary as the two guys headed back along the hard shoulder and eventually went out of sight behind the over bridge. Instead of roving guards, we positioned static sentries, and the remainder of the night passed without incident. As I lay trying to get off to sleep, I thought about how close I came to being responsible for making the decision to take their lives. And I wondered if those guys knew how close to death they had come tonight.

I woke frequently throughout the night. Perhaps because I knew we remained fairly vulnerable in our current location. Well before first light, I was up and packing my kit away. I was glad to see the first crack of light. Almost as soon as there was light the traffic started along the highway, a steady stream in both directions. I called the vehicle commanders together and reminded them that from here on in to the Green Zone was going to be a nonstop trip to include a night move through the northwest sector of the capital. But first we had the daytime trip along Highway 1, passing the northern suburbs of Fallujah. I moved Lima to the rear of the convoy to support Bravo and to keep traffic coming from our rear to the outside lanes in an attempt to keep the two inner lanes clear for the trucks. Foxtrot and Romeo provided mutual support at the front, and Sierra, we moved slightly ahead to check the culverts and underpasses as best we could in the time we had. The two Humvees that had rejoined us just before we headed off travelled a few hundred metres to our front.

The highway ran west to east and was raised about 10 metres above the surrounding area. Off to either side of the highway were bund lines about 2 metres high, running parallel. Ideal ambush firing points, I thought. Every hundred metres or so there was an underpass, large enough to drive a vehicle under. After several of these it was getting quite tiring scrambling up and down the sandy embankments. The convoy was cracking on between ten to twelve kilometres per hour, and Sammy and I were beginning to pay lip service as we quickly scanned the underpasses. Quite frankly we were going to have to be really lucky to spot any potentially hidden roadside IED. But I have always believed that you make your own luck. After scrambling back up from about the tenth underpass, the convoy was almost upon us and I was about the tell Sammy we would check every other one. The next, however, was a little further than normal, so I decided we would give it the once-over. As usual Sammy ran down the embankment on the approach side of the underpass, and I ran over and down the far side. I scanned the ground as I went. There was the normal roadside debris of car parts and burnt-out tyres. By the time I had ran down the embankment Sammy had already scanned under the road and was most of the way across the underpass. Sammy then stopped and bent down.

He had spotted a small loop of cable protruding out from the sand about an inch long. He hooked his finger under it and began to pull.

'STOP!' I shouted, and Sammy froze.

As he had pulled, more and more wire came from under the sand, leading right towards me. By the time I had shouted and Sammy reacted, there was about 2 metres free.

'Command wire,' I whispered. Why I whispered, I do not know, but then immediately thought of the oncoming convoy. I pictured some bastard hiding behind one of the bunds a few hundred metres away, just waiting to send an electric current down the wire to frag the convoy. I then also quickly pictured some of his mates about to open up on Sammy and me with small arms.

I saw Sammy raise his hand to his radio, I guessed to stop the convoy.

'No, RF hazard,' I said, putting up my hand to Sammy. By transmitting a radio near a wire, it is possible to induce a current that could be sufficient to set off a detonator. I signalled to Sammy to follow me and headed about 15 metres off to the side behind a raised piece of ground. We were now out of any direct line of sight of any potential small arms fire.

'All station, STOP, STOP, STOP. Potential command wire found under culvert,' I said over the radio in a clear and concise manner. I then spent about five seconds going through my combat appreciation. This is your thought process of weighing up all the factors and quickly coming up with your plan. To verbalise out loud would take at least twenty minutes, but in your head it takes seconds.

'OK, Bravo, stop all vehicles coming from the rear. Foxtrot, all-round defence to front of convoy. Romeo and Lima, scout 200 metres either side of axis for potential firing point. Sierra, provide local cover as I see what we have. Bravo, acknowledge me last,' I said, requiring Bravo as the furthest vehicle away to confirm he had heard and understood my snap orders over the radio.

'Roger, out,' replied Chalky in a crisp and precise acknowledgement.

Bearing in mind that as a team we had not worked much together, I could not help but be impressed at the way the guys reacted. Looking back towards the convoy, in the far distance, I could see Chalky and his guys out on foot, stopping the traffic. Martin had his guys out at the front of the convoy and taking up fire positions. Dom in Lima and Ray in Romeo raced forward and dismounted to start scouting the bund lines. In pairs the guys moved forward, leap-frogging each other.

I turned my radio off and said to Sammy to relay any info I gave him. I moved back to the wire. I took out my Leatherman tool and, separating the two core wires, cut each strand individually. By cutting both together you can always complete a circuit. My mind was racing, thinking of all the training I'd had. Collapsing circuit, I thought, but too sophisticated for this. (You can also initiate a detonator by cutting a current, but this would apply to more sophisticated setups.) I pulled at the cable going away from the embankment, and it snaked off perpendicular to the road. I pointed my arm off in its direction and shouted to Sammy, 'Main threat of firing point.' Sammy relayed the info over the radio, and I then tell Dom and Ray to re-direct their teams in that direction.

Now I tried to second-guess what anyone at the potential firing point would be thinking. They will have seen me and Sammy finding the wire. They will see eight men moving in their direction in a coordinated and well-trained manner. If I were them, I would push the tit to blow the IED, maybe rattle off a few rounds and withdraw into Fallujah to have a go another day. I had cut their wire, so no bang. The guys were now about 200 metres off the road, so any firing point would be not far off their effective range for small arms. My conclusion was that they had fled.

I now had a bit of a dilemma. Normally, the US Military EOD teams would be called, and they could take up to two to three hours to deal with this. To date, I was aware that roadside IEDs had consisted of converted artillery shells as they were plentiful, easily available, and simple to rig with a command wire into the nose end. I was also conscious that the convoy now stuck out like a sore thumb on the raised highway and was very vulnerable. So I made a decision and told Sammy, 'Request EOD via Davina.' But in the time it would take for them to arrive I would try and locate the actual device, any secondary devices, and see if I could render them safe so EOD would just have to blow them. This would save us a lot of time sitting around. I also assessed that this was a good opportunity to prove ourselves and set our reputation in Iraq.

I lay down on the ground and cleared my mind. All I needed to do was to trace the wire to the devise and uncover it. It would either be hidden under some roadside debris or buried slightly, but would be just off the side of the road. I pulled slowly at the wire and inched my way up the embankment towards the roadside. The wire pulled easily from beneath the sand, but every now and again there was resistance, and more force would be needed. I followed it 10 metres up the bank and eventually reached the top. There was about 2 metres from the shoulder of the embankment to the curbstone on the side of the road. A crash barrier ran just above the curbstone, and there was lots of debris. I kept pulling and kept inching forward, but slowed my pace as I neared to curb. As it was sand I did not need any tools and was able to dig and scrape with my bare fingers. Directly under the crash barrier there was a piece of burnt tyre about 20 centimetres wide and about 40 centimetres long. The radial coils were rusted and had been around for some time.

I slowly slid my fingers underneath it and gently levered it upwards.

'There you are, you little sod,' I muttered under my breath as I saw the nose of the 155 millimetre artillery shell just sticking out of the sand, the wires disappearing into the nose cone. I gently removed the piece of tyre and laid it off to the side. Then an image of my daughter and son playing in a paddling pool in the rear garden flashed into my mind. Fuck, I thought. What the fuck are you doing? I asked myself. You don't need to be doing this. Doubt crept in, and I inched back a bit. I had not told my family that I was going into Iraq, and as far as they were concerned I was safe and well in the ops room in Kuwait. The inner voice then started again. Come on, you know what you are doing. All you have to do is expose the shell so EOD can blow it. I inched forward again and started scraping the sand away with my fingers. But as sand does, it flowed back in as soon as I moved it. I placed the backs of my hands on the ground a few inches away from the shell and began to dig my fingers in at about a 45 degree angle, wiggling them as they dug in. I felt my fingertips touch the underside of the shell. I levered back on my elbows, and slowly the shell lifted, and the sand flowed underneath it. I was now holding the shell about an inch off the ground. I pivoted around my elbows and rotated the shell away from the small hole in the ground from whence it came. Gently I lowered it to the ground. It was then that I could see that the wire going into the nose cone came out again and led off along the roadside. A secondary device, I guessed. 'Bugger.'

Using my Leatherman I again cut the wires, so there was about six inches left. I shouted down to Sammy there was a secondary device, and he relayed it on. I again pulled gently at the wire, and slowly it unearthed. I inched forward on my stomach, following the wire. At each bit of debris I stopped and made a fingertip search, feeling under each piece. After about 20 metres I could see the ground had been disturbed recently. On top was another piece of tyre. I gently and slowly removed it and placed it off to the side. I could not see anything else, but the wires appeared to go straight down, and when I pulled they would not give. I slowly began brushing the sand aside with my fingertips. Then I felt the solid outer casing of another 155 millimetre artillery shell. Then I could hear someone quietly humming the Phil Collins song 'In the Air Tonight' and realised it was actually me. I stopped and said out loud, 'That's weird.' This shell was buried deeper than the first, so I needed to dig my fingers down at a steeper angle and go deeper to get underneath it. As my fingers wiggled deeper, the sand became denser, and I could feel it forcing its way underneath my finger nails. One or two smarted a bit, but not too painful. Once I got my fingertips underneath I again slowly lifted, and again the sand flowed underneath until it was clear of the ground. I pivoted and placed the shell down to the side. I cut the wires again to about 6 inches. I could not see any other wires leading off, but to make sure I pushed my hand down into the sand about a foot away from where the shell had been buried and began to circle around. I satisfied myself there was not another wire leading off. Based on the intelligence I had been given at the Sapper cell in Ramadi, there were normally two shells detonated at the rear of the convoy and another two at the front about 500 metres further on. But we needed to deal with this pair first. I got to my feet and walked about another 50 metres further on, looking for any disturbed ground. Seeing nothing untoward, I climbed over the crash barrier and walked back along the road. As I passed the two shells, I could see that they were now accessible to the little EOD remote vehicle they used.

By the time I had walked back to the front of the convoy it had taken about twenty-five minutes so far. I was informed EOD would be here in about another thirty minutes. I figured that they would then take about another hour to deal with both shells. I decided to try and speed up their task and make it easier for them. I walked back to the first shell. Sammy followed, and as I knelt down by it he took a photo.

'One for the scrapbook,' he said.

'OK,' I replied. 'I'm going to move this one and place it next to the other so EOD can just blow both together.'

I gently picked up the shell and walked over to the other one and placed it next to it. Sammy followed down and placed three stones on the curb just on the roadside to identify their location. Good thinking, I thought.

Just as we got back to the convoy again, EOD turned up. I explained what we had found and what I had done. I further explained that I was a former British EOD officer. I did this not to brag but to try and give these guys the confidence that what they were dealing with was relatively safe. I say relatively safe as I remembered a quote from an old EOD instruction manual, which went something like this: 'EOD Operators are reminded that in rendering safe an unexploded ordnance there is no one safe method, only one considered least dangerous.'

They deployed their little remote vehicle equipped with a camera. We watched on the monitor, and I thought that with this any 12-year-old kid could now deal with bombs. The operator directed straight to Sammy's mound of stones. From there they could clearly see the two shells sat side by side, exposed, just waiting to be blown. One of the EOD team donned a bomb suit and went forward with a charge of C4 to place on the shells. Within seconds he was on his way back. He had set some safety fuse burning, and shortly after his return to us, BANG. Up went the shells.

'You dug them out with your hands?' asked one of the EOD team.

'Well, you guys were late for two world wars, so we thought we would get on with it,' came Matt as quick as a flash.

I laughed and said, 'Be safe, guys,' and headed off to Sierra.

I was aware that potentially about several hundred metres further on was another IED. But fortunately, our route was taking us across the highway and off along a track about thirty degrees away. I had discussed this with the EOD team leader and so was confident that they would check this out.

The traffic had built up a lot behind us, and we now struggled to keep the traffic back while the convoy turned left across the highway. It took some aggressive posturing by some of the guys to make the civilian population wait until we were clear.

'OK, guys, we're clear of that, but about a klick up ahead we have a steel bridge to cross over a canal. Another vulnerable point, so keep it switched on,' I briefed over the radio. We were now on a gatched track slowly diverging away from the highway. A couple of hundred metres from the bridge Bravo and Lima went ahead to clear traffic so we could go straight over without stopping. It was quite clear and only a short bridge. Within ten minutes both trailers were over and no incidents. We now doglegged onto an RPG alley, which ran for about 40 kilometres in a dead-straight line, with waterways running either side. I again gave a warning over the radio to keep alert.

As we could not operate off to the flanks, I put Lima to the rear and kept Romeo at the front. We settled into our places and headed off down RPG Alley. After only a few hundred metres a distinctive crumple, the sound of a large explosion not too far off in the distance. I looked over my right shoulder and about a klick away saw a plume of black smoke rising. I figured it came from the vicinity of the high way and would have been at about the point the second set of IED would be. I only hoped it was a controlled explosion by the EOD Team. The mood was sombre as we carried on.

It was midafternoon and we were due to meet up with the Fourth Infantry Division, who were to provide some additional escorts into Baghdad itself. The RV was at the far end of RPG Alley, and we had forty kilometres to go at about ten kilometres per hour. I wanted to reach the RV before last light, so it was going to be tight. The Scammells chugged away, and we maintained a steady speed. On the recce we had been subjected to a few speculative shots, but now we were travelling at a much slower speed. After about 10 kilometres I could see that Romeo had dismounted and appeared to be searching a car. There was a crowd of about twenty adult males, and the road had widened with what appeared to be small lay-bys on either side of the road. Lima was also dismounting, and I saw their weapons being brought up to their shoulders. Something was up.

Sammy sped up, and Sierra quickly closed on the scene. The tension was immediately evident. Gareth had a man pinned against the side of the vehicle. Ray was looking in the boot of the car.

'I saw what I think was an RPG being put into the boot,' explained Gareth.

'And look what we have here,' shouted out Ray as he produced from the boot four AKs. A few of the males stepped forward, and Dom's team immediately shouted for them to get back and pointed their weapons at them.

The convoy was about 200 metres back but closing. The law of the land was that each adult male could have one AK-47 and one magazine.

'Any sign of an RPG?' I asked Ray.

'No' was his reply.

We had no right to remove weapons from Iraqis, and we had seen many armed so far. I did not want to stop the convoy, but we could not just hand over the weapons and carry on.

'OK, Dom, mount up your team and crack on ahead. Ray you hold this lot under cover,' I said. I picked up the AKs and walked about 20 metres along the road and laid them off to the side of the road. I walked back, being watched all the time by the crowd.

I turned to the man pinned against the car. 'You speak English?' I asked.

'Little,' he replied.

'OK, Gareth, let him go,' I told Gareth, and the man was released. I lowered my weapon and said to him, 'My friend, there is no problem here. We go past. When we gone, you take back your weapons. Understand?'

'Yes, I understand,' he replied. His face was full of hate, and I think if he could, he would have shot me dead right there. I tried to remain nonaggressive and smiled.

'Ray, keep this lot covered while the convoy rolls past. Once it's clear, mount up and follow on. Just be careful you don't drive over the AKs on the side of the road. Know what I mean,' I said with a knowing wink.

'Roger that,' Ray replied.

Just as Sierra mounted and headed off, the convoy caught up. As it did, both Foxtrot and Bravo also kept eyes on the crowd. As the convoy moved on, the Romeo team walked backwards, weapons at the ready. Once the convoy was about a hundred metres further on, they mounted up and sped off, 'accidentally' driving over the AKs, rendering them inoperative. Well, that's four out of commission, probably only about three million to go, I thought.

The whole incident had not slowed the convoy, and just as darkness was approaching we reached the RV. It was about 5 kilometres short of the meat market, where we would enter the outskirts of Baghdad. Davina again sprang into life and began barking orders at the troops. After a flurry of activity and repositioning of some Humvees, we had a get-together with the US Military for a briefing. Their senior guy was a fresh-faced captain who explained that the Fourth Infantry Div would provide a rolling outer cordon over the two nights we would take to cross Bagdad. There was a general curfew in place, so we would not expect any traffic or people out on the streets. He explained that we would not move for another two hours until the curfew had taken effect. I briefed my guys and told them to have a good meal and, if possible, get an hour's kip. We were going to be walking all night through to the Green Zone.

I managed a ten-minute power nap and felt much better for it. I took my boots and socks off for a while to give my feet an airing and munched on something that tasted quite nice from an MRE.

The captain gave a wave, and we headed off. He had stated they had a lot of cover out. I could see a minimum of ten Humvees, but we were still in quite a restrictive location. As we approached the meat market and the streets opened up, I was impressed to see armoured personnel carriers and even a main battle tank. Then, overhead I heard a helicopter approaching. It was a small one, and I guessed it was for command and control rather than to provide any form of firepower.

The route from the northwest corner of Baghdad into the Green Zone had many turns, so the convoy did not pick up any speed. Not that I considered 10 kilometres per hour speed, but it crawled along at about 2 kilometres per hour. We formed the walking cordon, and for the most part the streets were quite wide, and we were able to spread out. I walked point along the centre of the road. Sammy drove Sierra about 10 metres behind me, and Nigel and Matt were off to my sides. Lima and Romeo moved back around the convoy and walked either side of it. As we moved, the military were manoeuvring along the streets running parallel to us. They provided a pretty sterile zone around us, and I felt quite reassured. They appeared to move in a well-coordinated manner, and I was impressed.

As we went deeper into Baghdad the density of buildings increased and our fields of vision reduced. If anything were to happen, we would have to react pretty quickly. After about three hours we reached the elevated road where James had previously walked up, and on approach, I could see that a team was busily removing the central barrier so the convoy could swing around and back down the other side. It was pretty slick, and the convoy never slowed, which was just as well, as we were again exposed, with the road level being equal with surrounding rooftops. We continued heading southeast towards the Green Zone situated in a bend of the Tigris River. Another three hours later I could see the high perimeter wall. Again a flurry of activity went on as a crane removed sections of the wall to allow the convoy through into the Green Zone. It was nearly daylight, and we had been walking the convoy in for nearly seven hours. I could see the guys were knackered, and I too was looking forward to a lie-down and rest my weary bones. It was a choke point like this that I expected an incident, as the troops would have been preparing to remove the wall sections for an hour or two before and would have drawn attention that something was going to happen at that very point. The morning traffic was starting as the curfew had lapsed. But without incident the convoy crawled through the gap in the wall, and it was quickly closed behind us.

We pulled the convoy up along the side of the road within the Green Zone just short of a large pair of swords going over the road, a former symbol of Saddam's rule.

'OK, the military want to run over the route we will take tonight,' Davina informed me, just as I was looking forward to some sleep. We have been on the go for about twenty-seven hours. It was not just to talk over the route; they wanted to drive it. I decided that I for one would rather get it done and then have some uninterrupted sleep. James agreed. So we mounted up a couple of vehicles and headed for the south gate over the Fourteenth of July Bridge. The traffic was really heavy as we swung east towards the Army Canal road. With a few Humvees pushing their way, though, we made good progress.

As we reached the Army Canal Road there was a sandy strip of land running parallel, which we had to cross. A lot of civil works had been done to prepare a compacted route across. The military guys dismounted, and we spent several minutes looking at it. James cast his eye over it and gave the thumbs up. Like me, he had also assessed that the more we paid attention to this piece of ground, the more attention we drew, and it was an ideal location to bury a nasty surprise. With some cajoling, we managed to get the troops mounted up and moved on towards Al Quds Power Station. We returned to the Green Zone, and I couldn't help feeling that the unit that would escort us tonight would not be as slick as last night.

Back in the Green Zone, I found myself a bunk bed within the prayer room of Saddam's former palace and managed to set my alarm before I crashed into a deep sleep. Too knackered even for my mind to go racing over tonight's move.

I gave myself plenty of time to have a good shower and to shave off a pathetic attempt at a beard. Also a hearty meal before we formed up, ready to move out for the second night's move across Baghdad. After a quick briefing with the guys and a check of weapons, I headed off across the Fourteenth of July Bridge ... or rather a rickety old steel bridge running down just off to the side. I was a little dismayed to see that there were flood lights and lots of troops milling around. Not armed troops, but a lot of brass and media. Cameras and video cameras. The US Military were going to make as much publicity out of this as possible and no doubt would be appearing in Stars and Stripes (the US Army's magazine). I looked along the line of buildings heading off east along the riverbank and could see figures in the windows. Obviously interested in what was going on. But also could be a possible sniper.

The convoy crept slowly over the bridge and with lots of snaps and video footage collected, the media scrum withdrew back over the bridge into the Green Zone. It all became peaceful, and we shook out into our walking cordon and headed along the road parallel to the river.

James approached me and asked, 'Can I have a radio for Davina? She would like to be able to listen in to you guys.'

'Sure,' I replied and handed him a spare from my vehicle. 'I guess her call sign can be Alpha,' I said with a smile on my face. James burst out laughing. 'Alpha for army, I mean.' It had become a bit of a joke that the guys had starting referring to Davina as the Alpha Male as she appeared to jump into action whenever we were with troops and as she was the only female on the convoy.

As we headed east the Ministry of Electricity had a team out, and every time we came to an overhead wire, then deployed a ladder and tried to push the wires up so the convoy could pass under. At first this was not too much of a problem, but it did slow progress. Then as we moved further on, the wires appeared to increase, until progress was halted.

'Ali, surely all these wires cannot be legal ones,' I asked in a leading way.

'Oh no, Mr Mike, most of these are put up by residents stealing electricity,' he replied.

'So it won't be a problem if they get ripped down?' I again asked in a leading way. 'James, will it be a problem if the turbine rips the wires down?' I asked.

'Not at all, dear chap. Won't even notice it,' James replied.

'Full steam ahead then,' I ordered.

'Right you are, sir,' James replied with a smile on his face as he headed back to the lead tractor. Within a hundred metres it was like a ticker tape parade, with overhead wires ripping from poles and houses and draping over the turbine. The trailer crews were busily pulling off the wires, assisted by the Ministry of Electricity team.

I was happier we were now making some headway. I then became aware that there was a complete absence of troops. The streets had been full of military vehicles a short time ago, and I was thankful as we appeared to have as good a support as last night. What became apparent was that this lot had formed a static cordon around us, and as we moved into the cordon, they upped sticks and moved a couple of klicks and went firm again. So at times we were outside of the cordon, obviously not as well coordinated as their comrades last night. Just as I was feeling a little vulnerable, I could hear a commotion to the rear. Over the radio I heard Chalky. 'Stand to, stand to, vehicle approaching from rear at speed.'

I looked back and could see guys dashing for cover and taking up fire positions. Approximately 100 metres further back along the riverbank I could see a small car heading at speed towards the convoy. Suicide bomber? I thought. But so far this was not a tactic that had been used. I then saw Matt Williams step into the road and stand with his weapon raised and his left hand up in a halt sign. Immediately the car began to slow and came to an abrupt halt about 20 metres short of Matt. Within seconds Chalky and a couple of the guys had moved in and had the occupants covered. Two figures emerged from the vehicle with their hands raised. They were young males, probably late teens. They were quickly pushed to the floor and searched. By the time I had made my way by foot to the rear of the convoy, Chalky declared, 'No weapons found.'

The two young lads looked terrified. Ali appeared at my side and started shouting at them. After a short exchange, Ali informed me that they had just bought the car that day and wanted to go out for a ride. I guess it was like any other young buck anywhere else in the world with a new car. Hardly new, as it was a beat-up old light blue Opel Kadett, complete with a German registration plate. I had seen a lot of car transporters coming in from Jordan laden with German-registered cars. For years young men were not allowed cars, so now this was a new thing, and these two were out for a joyride. A couple of Humvees appeared, and we handed them over to the military. After all, they were breaking the curfew and not for us to deal with.

As I walked back to the front of the convoy I felt proud that the guys had dealt with the incident in a controlled and professional way. They could have simply filled the approaching car with lead and no one would have brought them to book over it. But I thought to myself, Good, controlled British squaddie, well done.

After about 600 metres we turned right and then left onto what everyone called Tottenham Court Road. By day this was a busy shopping street, but tonight it was empty and wide, and we managed to make good progress. As we headed towards the outskirts of eastern Baghdad we made several turns along backstreet. As I walked down the centre of the road, Sammy was in the vehicle about 10 metres, Matt was to my left, and Nigel was off to my right. The convoy was about 50 metres further back, and the guys were walking either side. It was about 0200 hrs, and the streets were very quiet. The military had just done one of their skips forward and were nowhere to be seen or heard.

Suddenly from an alleyway to my forward left a male appeared with an AK. He was carrying it in his left hand and holding it by the stock. I immediately dropped to one knee and put the butt of my weapon to my shoulder. He froze. He clearly did not expect to see me standing in the middle of the road. His eyes darted either side of the street and clocked both Matt and Nigel. Was he a bad guy and was about to bring his weapon to bear? Would he stand a chance, with three of us ready to shoot back? Was he thinking whether he had enough time to shoot at all three of us? Or was he just another young lad sneaking home under curfew? After all, all Iraqi adult males were allowed to possess an AK. He was breaking the law by being out under curfew, but he just did not seem like a threat. There was no way he would have time to swing the weapon around into a firing position and get some rounds off. I smiled and slowly stood up. I raised my left hand and waved him on. He smiled back and as he turned to head off I heard him whisper in a rather loud way, 'Thank you, Mister.' Would he at some time in the future kill or attempt to kill someone? I don't know, but he was not an immediate threat to me or the convoy. Within seconds he was gone.

The whole incident took about fifteen very tense seconds but did not slow the convoy. As it continued to wind through the street, ripping out wires, the darkness of the streets were periodically lit up by the sparks of the wires arcing as they were pulled away. Ironically, we were transporting in a generator and turbine to increase their power supply, but here we were, ripping out their wires.

We approached the Army Canal Road perpendicular and first had to cross the strip of sand we had looked at earlier the previous day. It was about 50 metres wide, and I knew we had about two minutes to have a visual check to see if there was any disturbed sand where an IED could have been concealed. Just the other side of Army Canal Road was Sadr City, a no-go area for the military and within view of our crossing point. I could see a military presence on the far side, but they appeared to be moving further on. Sammy and I quickly scanned the route over and satisfied ourselves that there was nothing there. Satisfied or tried to convince ourselves? Within no time the convoy was upon us, and over it trundled. Sierra Team crossed the Army Canal Road and onto the service road running along the front edge of Sadr City. We all knew this was a likely hot spot.

As the lead trailer turned left onto the service road, a sudden burst of automatic gun fire came from about 200 metres ahead. 'Stand to,' I shouted. There was a roar from an armoured vehicle, so I knew the military was close. The last thing I wanted was for me or any of the guys to go running forward to see what was happening. There was no obvious fire coming in our direction, so we remained still. After about thirty seconds I stood up and moved forward. There was a slight bend in the road, and as I walked forward I could see flashes of light but could not hear any gunshots. The flashes did not seem right. They were more like the flash from the overhead wires being ripped out. As I cautiously walked around the bend I could see a small car that had crashed into the wall to the right of the road. To its rear was an APC (armoured personnel carrier) with about ten soldiers milling around. Another flash. As I walked closer I could also hear laughter. The troops appeared totally oblivious that I, a civilian who was armed, was approaching. I was not a threat to them, but I would have thought they would at least have someone keeping an eye out. Especially as we were on the edge of what they had told me was a 'no go area for US Military'.

As I drew near I could see that the windscreen of the car was smashed. Then in the darkness, another flash, and in an instant the inside of the car was illuminated, revealing a chilling scene. Sat in the driver's seat was a young adult male. His face covered in blood and a large hole in the left upper chest area. I assumed the burst of machine gun fire had neatly grouped the rounds, causing a fatal burst. The left side of his neck was pretty much missing, giving the appearance his head was nearly blown off his shoulders. Sat in the passenger seat was a young soldier who had slid into the car and had pulled the dead guy's arm up over his shoulder. As he struck a pose with his war trophy, his mate had taken a photo. As I stood in amazement another soldier pulled at his mate in the passenger seat. 'C'mon, give me a turn.' The two soldiers duly swapped places and another flash went to capture the moment. It was like a photo booth as they all took turns.

'What the fuck,' I exclaimed as I saw a captain approaching on foot. Then I saw that between the car and the APC, lying on his front with his arms plasticuffed to his rear, was another young male. No one appeared to be watching him. I listened in as a soldier explained to the captain that the car had driven down the road and that the machine gunner on the APC had put a burst through the windscreen at the driver. It was further established that the car had not been speeding and that no attempt to wave it down or warn it was made. No weapons had been found, but both males had German passports. The survivor was saying the odd German word and would not reply to an Arabic translator who was trying to talk to him. By now some of my guys had also closed in, and I could hear the lead trailer rumbling closer. It was clear the very young captain was now totally unsure of what to do next as his troops looked on, awaiting instructions. After an uneasy silence I turned to one of my guys who had married a German girl while serving in Germany. He spoke fluent German. He spoke to the guy on his belly and after a short while declared that while the survivor did speak a small amount of German, he could not 'spreken it enough, and he isn't German'.

'OK, cut them off and let him go,' instructed the

captain.

'What?' I angrily asked. 'If your guys thought the car was sufficient enough threat to open up and shoot him dead and you got this guy with a dodgy German passport, I would suggest to you, Captain, that at least take him in for some questioning. Don't you, Captain?' I was pissed off at how unprofessional and childish the whole incident was being handled. I know that in the heat of the moment a split-second decision could make the difference. But it appeared the US troops believed themselves unaccountable for their actions. This young lad had a family, and tonight he would not be coming home. There probably would be no explanation as to how he was killed. And no one would be asked to justify why they shot first and asked questions later.

I realised I was stood toe to toe with the captain and there was tension in the air. 'Boss, the convoy is coming through,' I heard Matt say.

'Yeah, OK. Let's crack on,' I replied. As I turned and walked away I maintained eye contact with the captain until he dropped his gaze downwards. I felt I had made my point but thought it unlikely to have any impact.

I had lost track of how long this incident had taken but guessed several minutes. I was keen as always to keep the convoy moving, especially because of our proximity to Sadr City. We had about another kilometre to run along its southwest edge before we headed north on Route 2, a four-lane highway where we could pick up some speed. We shook out into our walking cordon again, and without the trailers stopping we pushed on past the corpse and the prisoner being put into a Humvee. After a flurry of activity from the military vehicles, we were again left on our own. Somehow I felt a little safer without this unit around me. I could not help ponder the difference in standards between the two units. Last night they were slick, well coordinated, and professional. It was chalk and cheese.

Dawn was approaching as we picked up some speed and mounted our vehicles. We repositioned the vehicles into our normal pattern, and Sammy and I reverted to jumping in and out of the wagon to check culverts. As we headed north along Route 2, the built-up area fell away, and open countryside was either side. I was happier with this, as our fields of view were better and provided less hiding places for ambush. Along the left side of the highway was a canal with tall reeds. Every now and again there were small settlements of what I guessed were family groups. They lived in latterly straw huts and, with a few chickens and the odd goat, appeared to live a very basic existence. The kids were in rags and stared with big brown eyes at us as we moved by. There were no outstretched arms begging for food, even though they all looked malnourished. There was also a real sadness about them. 'Weapons of mass destruction or not, this is good enough reason to have come in,' Matt said. I looked at him, and he was welling up. I don't know if it was tiredness and emotion that we were nearing the end of this job, but there was a real sense of sorrow for what I can only describe as these peasants living in amongst the reeds along the bank of this canal.

Not wanting anyone to switch off on the last few kilometres, I said over the radio, 'OK, guys, we have a couple of klicks to go. Let's keep sharp.' The sun was up, and there was a heavy mist over the fields either side of the highway. After about 10 kilometres we turned left across the other side of the dual carriageway and headed along a narrower road across the fields towards Al Quds Power Station. A few klicks later we saw the welcoming committee at the gates. Bob and his security team were all waiting. I dismounted from my wagon and stood by the gates. I stood and watched as the convoy rolled in. There was a look of satisfaction on the guys' faces. As the rear trailer entered that gate I could see Shukla sitting on his seat, still wearing his helmet and visor and a huge beaming smile. We had done it. We had escorted a generator and gas turbine nearly 800 kilometres across Iraq, through Baghdad, and all arrived safely and intact.

Personally, I felt a huge amount of satisfaction. In a matter of days I had managed to assemble a team and equipment to deploy into Iraq. It was rushed and I would have liked more preparations. I would have liked better equipment, maps, etc., but there was simply not enough time or they were not available. In all of my working life, the past two weeks had given me the most satisfaction. We were not in the Army, so the guys did not have to listen to me because I held the Queen's commission. I genuinely felt I had led the convoy well and the guys respected and followed me because they wanted to. I was conscious that the mission was not over. We still had to escort the empty ALE trailers and crew back to Jordan and then get our team back to Kuwait.

The trailers and crew remained at Al Quds to offload, and we returned to the Green Zone without incident. After a good day and night's rest we returned to Al Quds early the following day. With the trailers empty we headed off at normal speed and by the end of the day had travelled along the highways around Baghdad and back to the Jordanian border. We stayed overnight at the border and the next day travelled back up to BIAP. After a night's stopover and some good stodge in the cookhouse we headed south to Kuwait.

We arrived late afternoon, and now for a real test. How were we going to fare getting back into Kuwait with all the arms and ammunition? We stopped short of the crossing point and stashed the weapons as best we could under the rear seat of the Nissan Patrols. Those who had pistols kept them handy. As we approached the Kuwaiti Army checkpoint I slipped my pistol down behind the ceramic chest plate of my body armour. All five vehicles pulled up, and we all got out and opened all doors as to invite a full inspection and to say, 'We have nothing to hide.' It worked. A Kuwaiti captain strolled around the vehicles, making cursory glances in. After about a minute he nonchalantly waved his hand and headed back to his hut. We loaded up and headed the kilometre further on to the search bays, where the US Military were waiting. This was going to be tougher. Again we all stepped out and invited the search. A soldier lifted a few bags in the rear compartment of the wagons and simply looked into the crew compartments. I guess they were not too worried whether we had anything or not. We were waved on, and into Kuwait we drove.

Mission complete, or at least that was what I thought. As we neared the villa, one of the wagons misjudged his braking distance and bumped into the rear of one of our other wagons. Thank God it was all in-house and no vehicles were badly damaged.

It was dark as we pulled into the rear yard of the villa. Steve, Shep, and the ops room staff all came out to greet us. Lots of smiles all round. 'OK, you lot, let's get the vehicles unloaded and inside,' came some shouting from a bald-headed guy in his fifties.

'Who the fuck are you?' I asked.

'Dave. Dave Hill,' he replied.

'Well, nice to meet you, Dave Hill, but these aren't kids, and they know what needs doing,' I snapped back as I walked past and up to Steve. 'And?' I asked Steve, knowing all too well he would have brought this guy on without telling me.

'He's an ex-captain RA, and he's on board as a watch keeper,' replied Steve, with a look of disbelief on his face. Steve had this way of making people feel they were being unreasonable when in fact it was he who had done something without thinking it through or consultation.

'Well, thanks for letting me know,' I said as I turned

to unload my kit from the wagon. It was not so much that this guy was shouting at the guys because he was right that we needed to get the kit inside and sorted and right now was the time the guys would switch off. It was more that he was shouting at my guys, my team that had been together for the past few weeks, and I did not want anyone else shouting at my guys. I had to take a step back and tell myself not to be so possessive. Dave was carrying out the sergeant major bit, and I guess it was as good a way as any for him to 'introduce' himself to the guys. Shep, on the other hand, went about it in a quieter manner, going around shaking hands and welcoming the guys back.

Without any further prompting, the guys dumped their kit bags on the floor of the basement and went about cleaning their weapons and emptying their magazines. The smell of gun oil was soon overtaken by the smell wafting out from the kitchen, as a hearty meal was being prepared. 'Oh-nine-hundred tomorrow, guys, for debrief,' I shouted as I headed up the stairs to my room. I was not heading to my bed but something far more important; time to submit our first invoice.

I had prepared an invoice format before I had left. Now it was a simple case of inserting the daily rate times the number of men and the number of days up country. Kerching! The total amount came just short of three-quarters of a million dollars. Most of that would be eaten up by the first set of wages due at the end of January, but there would be a few hundred thousand left over. The good news was that there was going to be a second identical convoy in a few weeks. I duly e-mailed the invoice off to K+N and headed off for a long hot shower.

ANY OTHER BUSINESS

The following morning I held a debrief of the operation. All were generally happy at the way things went, and the main point that came out was weaponry. More specifically we needed newer weapons, as some were quite old. We also needed a lot more ammunition, especially 9 millimetres, as this was quite scarce. Following the debrief, I then got the guys in one at a time and spoke with them individually. I wanted to establish if there were any other issues they would want to raise within the group. Apart from one or two minor issues, I was also interested to see what the guys though about others in the team. There was the usual praise for mates and moans about one or two, but one person kept being mentioned. Matt Williams, a former Royal Welch fusilier, was mentioned by every single guy. They were not complimentary about his interpersonal skills, and all felt that he was close to being unhinged. He was part of Bravo Vehicle at the back of the convoy, and I had not seen much of him. I relied a lot on Chalky for his opinion, and I agreed that we could not risk having someone who was not a team player and the guys felt they could not rely on. He would not be invited back.

Another name that kept coming up was John Fisher. He was a former Royal Corps of Transport driver. When asked what the problem was, none of the guys could really express what it was, but every single one mentioned him. He was a little 'different' from the rest. He was a self-confessed Buddhist, which was a little strange to be doing work in armed security. Most of the guys were infantry, and to them a driver did not really cut the mustard. However, as I mentioned before, these drivers will have done this sort of convoy work on operations many times, and I was sure, if tested, he would hold his own. He was to stay.

Other useful information that dropped out was that Chalky and Ray Clarke came out well as potential team leaders. Both had their strengths in different ways, but the guys appeared to like them, and I needed to identify team leaders if we were to start running more than one operation at a time.

It was the last week of January now, and we were informed that the repeat convoy for the generator and turbine would be in two to three weeks' time. Steve was busy trying to follow some leads for more work. He had met a guy called Steve Whittle, who worked for Al-Bahar Shipping. They had the contract for supplying the Japanese camp in Samawah, which was about halfway to Baghdad. Due to the Japanese constitution, after the Second World War they were not allowed to have an army. So they had the Japanese Ground Self-Defense Force. They were not allowed to carry out any offensive action and could only defend themselves. So all their supplies being transported from Kuwait to Samawah on civilian trucks needed security, as they would not be allowed to take action should the convoy be attacked. We had a meeting with Steve Whittle and established that there was a convoy a week going to the camp. It was a day's run to the camp. The trailers would offload overnight, and then the empty trailers would run back the following day. There would be between six to ten trailers per convoy. This sounded like an ideal project. We discussed putting three escort vehicles with three guys in each vehicle. The area was fairly quiet regarding insurgent activity, and most incidents were of a criminal nature. We provisionally agreed a rate. All that was required was to meet the Japanese Military to convince them we knew what we were doing and get a green light.

The following day, Steve announced that his old regiment was disbanding and there was to be a parade in

Cardiff. He and Simon Adams would fly back to UK on Thursday and would be back the following Tuesday. I was rather glad Steve would be out of country, as I did not want him going to see the Japs. He has a habit of trying to talk about things he did not really know, and his large frame was really not what we wanted to portray to them. I decided to take Chalky with me, as I was going to need a team leader for this. I did not tell him of my intentions but just told him we were going to see the Japs to discuss possible convoy protection in principle.

We drove about half an hour out into the desert just outside Kuwait City to where the Japs had set up their camp. What struck me first was that all their uniforms and vehicles were green and not sandy coloured. We went into the command cell and were introduced to a colonel. His English was perfect, and we freely discussed how we intended to protect the convoy. Despite the lack of military experience due to their limited role, the colonel was a sharp cookie and asked all the relevant questions. He asked what we would do if the Japanese Military were attacked. I explained that we would assist. I asked him what the Japanese Military would do if we were attacked. He looked straight faced and said, 'You are on your own, and we cannot help.' There was a slight pause, and then he winked. I was not quite sure what he was implying, but having researched the Japanese Ground Self-Defense Force, I discovered the highlight of their training year was to build a house out of ice blocks in Northern Japan. So I was not expecting too much assistance in any case.

As we left the command cell and walked back to our vehicle, Chalky exclaimed, 'Bloody hell. I'm going to write a book about all this one day.' Chalky was a straight-up-and-down old-school sergeant, and he was clearly finding all this bizarre but intriguing.

On the drive back to the villa, I turned to Chalky and

said, 'Well, what do you think?'

'Piece of cake, really. Nice little number, up and down in two days, once a week,' he summarised.

'Good, 'cos I want you to lead this,' I replied. He looked at me with surprise. 'Yes, and you get a pay raise' I said as I rolled my eyes as if that would be the next question.

'Yeah, OK,' said Chalky.

'We can discuss a team for you, but put some thought to it,' I said. I could see out the corner of my eye he was preening at the thought of 'his team'. He deserved it.

All I had to do was to wait to get feedback from Steve Whittle on whether the Japs liked us. In the meantime, my thoughts turned to sourcing more weapons and ammo. I called my contact in Basra and arranged to meet outside the British Military logistics base at Shuaibah on the outskirts of Basra. We made a team of four vehicles and, the following day, headed over the border to meet up. My contact was a high-ranking member of the police and was able to source better weapons and lots of ammo. Again Chalky came in handy, as he was a weapons instructor, and gave the weapons on offer a good going over. There were some crap but also some good quality AKs. Also lots of ammo, and I mean lots. We came away with several grenades, 14 good-quality AKs, and 20,000 rounds of ammunition. He said he could get more, and we agreed to meet in a week's time.

We then headed across Basra to Saddam's palace on the banks of the Shatt al-Arab Waterway where the Royal Regiment of Wales were based. Matt Jones had, until recently, been a platoon sergeant with them. One of the quartermasters was a mate of his, and they were about to head back to UK at the end of their tour. We were given free run of his stores so filled the wagons with boots, pots and pans, rations, and anything else we thought useful and could fit in. After a quick stop off at the cook house and a bite to eat we also loaded several large packets of bacon into some cool boxes and headed off. The bacon would come in very handy as bargaining power. A good day's shopping, I thought.

By halfway through the next week I had turned my attentions to getting more guys out to Kuwait. I would need twenty for the next turbine convoy and nine for the Jap convoy, if it took off. Simon had returned after their disbandment parade, but Steve said he had to stay in the UK for some meetings. At first I was not concerned, but after a couple of days he was being very vague about what meetings he was having. We had agreed that we would generally plan to do six weeks in Kuwait and two weeks back in the UK. When back, I would continue to recruit, and he would develop business. But it was clear that the focal point of business development was going to be out in the Middle East. Already I was getting the feeling that Steve was going to be staying back in the UK as much as he could get away with.

I chased up Steve Whittle a few times, but he said he was still waiting for confirmation from the Japs. K+N was also being evasive over the start date of the next turbine convoy. I was holding off calling guys out as I already had fifteen in the country and was paying them each day. Thankfully, after another couple of days Steve Whittle called and wanted to sign up the contract. The Jap convoys were confirmed, and so Chalky chose his team.

Then K+N called us forward for the turbine convoy. I called forward extra guys from the UK and within two days had the complement of twenty required. Steve was still in the UK and making no signs of coming back out to Kuwait. The more I phoned him, the more evasive he became. It was now mid-February, and he had been back just over two weeks. We now had two contracts about to start, and we needed a director in the villa at all times. I spoke to Ray Clarke and asked him if he would want to lead the turbine convoy. He was up for it. I was a little apprehensive even though I knew he was more than capable of leading the team and the guys were all good. I was more concerned about the diplomatic liaison with clients out on the ground. We had set ourselves a good reputation, but we could easily lose it as well.

The first Jap convoy was important to us, as I believed this would be our main business: collecting convoys at the border and escorting them into Iraq. We had to get the process right as delays getting over the border could spell disaster. The likes of Al Bahar Shipping were freight forwarders who tried to coordinate things but did not actually have any assets. I saw an opportunity that if we took control of the border procedures of booking a trip ticket with the military and arranging the convoys, we could make ourselves invaluable. I requested a list of trucks from Steve so that we could book our slot over the border. To my amazement he sent a list of fifty trucks. We had previously discussed convoys of six to ten trailers. For this, three escort vehicles would have been enough. But for fifty trailers, it was nowhere near enough. It is not an exact science, but I assessed that I would want one vehicle at the front, one at the back, one as forward recce, and then one for every ten vehicles in the convoy. This meant for a convoy of fifty trailers, I would want seven escort vehicles. I demanded a meeting with Steve Whittle. I do not know if he was thinking that we would turn up with three escort vehicles and not notice there were fifty trailers.

We met that afternoon and thrashed out a contract, whereby he eventually agreed with my assessment of what was needed. However, it was agreed that the first convoy would only be twenty trailers. As it transpired it was not only supplies for the camp but also building materials. The Japs were in Samawah on a humanitarian mission and were there to help build the infrastructure of this small town. This still meant I needed more guys, more vehicles, and quickly.

I went back to the Nissan showroom, and to the surprise of Anwar the salesman, I ordered another three Nissan Patrols for cash. I also managed to get a 15 per cent discount, on the promise I would be ordering another three next week. By the end of the third week of February both the turbine convoy and Jap convoy teams were equipped and ready to deploy. Ray and his team headed off early one morning to Shep's advice to stay low, move fast, and trust no one. I felt mixed emotions of wanting to be on the convoy and slight guilt that I was staying in the safety of the villa. On reflection the stress of trying to ensure we were running a viable company was worse than going into the hostile environment of Iraq.

Two days later the first Jap convoy was ready to roll. We were deploying four escort vehicles with a total of twelve men. We were a man short, so I decided I would make up the numbers and told Chalky I was just a shooter and the team was his. I was also keen to complete the first of this sort of convoy to understand the potential problems that may exist. We arrived at the staging area about an hour before first light. Chalky went into the control room and booked the trip ticket for the convoy. The rest of us marshalled the trailers into a line ready to roll. Most of the drivers were Indian, and their supervisor appeared bewildered over a bunch of white guys with weapons herding them about. Our convoy was third in line. Lesson number 1: get someone up there earlier to book the first slot. There were no suitable stopping points for the convoy, and we would need all the daylight hours to reach the Jap camp on the outskirts of Samawah. If we were delayed getting over the border because of other convoys, we would face real problems.

Our time came, and we rolled over the border. The trailers moved a lot faster than we were used to after the turbine convoy, and before we knew it we had passed Safwan and were out on the main highway of Tamper heading north. It had three lanes on our side, and the convoy settled into the middle lane, and before long we were whistling along at 110 kilometres per hour. The convoy was fairly well spaced, but even with only twenty trucks, it was over 700 metres in length. I imagined that a convoy of fifty would be well over a kilometre front to back. Command and control was going to be difficult. Other civilian traffic was quite light, and as each car approached and overtook the convoy, one of the escort vehicles would shadow it the length of the convoy, to be known as sheepdogging. I was pleasantly surprised how quickly the guys adapted to this form of escorting. As we neared junctions, instinctively one vehicle would sprint forward and block it off to allow uninterrupted travel of the convoy. After about 170 kilometres we bared left off route Tamper onto a much narrower road heading for Samawah. There were no large built-up areas en route, just small villages every now and again. This road had only one lane in both directions, and overtaking was difficult. We were able to maintain a good speed of about 80 kilometres per hour, and by about 1500 hrs we were approaching Samawah. To the south of the town there was a fork in the road, and we headed off left again. After about another 2 kilometres we reached the camp.

The camp had high perimeter walls with machine gun posts at the corners. There was an elaborate chicane system on the approach to the main gate, which was difficult for the forty-foot flatbed trailers to negotiate. This made for slow progress getting the trailers into the camp. We formed a rear cordon to protect those trailers waiting out on the road. Once all were in we went to follow. To our amazement the Japs would not let us in. We were directed to a large open space to the east of the walled camp. This is where the empty trailers were sent after they had been offloaded. This was also to be our home for the night. Chalky quickly sorted out a perimeter guard, and we settled in for the night. Lesson number 2: be self-sufficient (which really we already knew).

After a night of taking turns on stag (guard duty) and not much sleep, we formed up for the return trip. The empty trailers moved even quicker on the way back, and without incident we approached the border after only a few hours. As we headed into the search lanes the trailers were filtered off one way, and our vehicles another for searching. After a cursory search we headed off for the villa. Invoice number 2 soon was on its way to Al Bahar Shipping.

Over the next few weeks Ray lead the turbine convoy successfully and without incident, and Chalky was running a convoy for the Japs to Samawah every couple of days. The invoices were flying out, and our bank account was beginning to look healthy. This was what we had set out to achieve, and it was looking good. However, Steve had now stretched the long weekend for his regimental disbandment parade into six weeks. When I left home on 26 December I told the wife and kids I would see them in about six weeks. It was now mid-March, and I felt Steve was now starting to take the piss. He was on his third marriage and had a small child, so I understood that he did not want to be away. But rather than come out straight and say so, he continued to maintain he had meetings arranged in UK but still nothing was forthcoming. We were starting to pick up a few other jobs from other freight forwarders in Kuwait, but these were the results of a meeting Steve and I had several months back.

We were instructed by Mishare that we must have either Steve or myself in Kuwait at all times. Steve was registered as the general manager in the Chamber of Commerce, and by Kuwaiti law, Mishare stated, he must not be out of the country for more than forty-five days in the year. He was fast approaching that on just this stretch. I was also running out of stories to tell Mishare about Steve's whereabouts. SO also started to ask questions.

As we picked up more work, I was running out of guys to call forward. I needed to get back to the UK to do some more recruiting. Eventually in the last week of March Steve flew back out. I planned a series of interviews for the next two weeks back in the UK and also a week's holiday with the family. Before I headed for the UK, we had a meeting of the four shareholders to assess progress. During the meeting Mishare asked Steve what his plans were for repaying the loan Mishare had made. I was astonished. After the meeting and Mishare had left the villa, I asked Steve what he meant by 'repaying the loan'.

'It was my understanding that Mishare had invested half a million dollars in SFI and for that he became a partner and agreed to 25 per cent profit share,' I said.

'And that was my understanding as well,' confirmed SO.

'It was always a loan we had to pay back,' replied Steve.

'I distinctly recall you explaining that it was Mishare's way of buying into the company and that we would all be equal-profit share,' reiterated S O.

'We have to pay back the half million first,' maintained Steve.

'So are you saying we have to pay back half a million dollars to Mishare before any others get to see some profit?' I asked, trying to keep my cool. I knew Steve could be economical with the truth and had a knack of looking all innocent when you knew damn well he was blagging it the Brierley way.

'Look, this is normal business practice, and I'm sure we will have paid him off in no time,' stated Steve.

'Steve, do you have any idea where we are on finances?' I asked.

'Diane will go over the books and tell us how we are

sitting,' replied Steve. Diane was his wife and an accountant.

'Well that will be great, but let me tell you we will have, after paying March wages, about two hundred grand left. With that we need to cover villa rent, flights, and we need a couple of new vehicles. We also need to be putting something into a savings account to cover annual insurance towards the end of the year, which will be the best part of a million,' I said, again trying to keep my cool.

'Look, if we can pay this back quickly, Mishare will see that SFI is worth something, and he will sell it to another Kuwaiti, and we all benefit,' announced Steve.

I was staggered at Steve's naivety and simply walked out of the room and headed to my bedroom to pack. Perhaps I was a little tired and needed to get back to the UK for a few weeks and regain perspective.

Before heading for the airport Steve suggested that he and I should tell Mishare that we had each put in forty thousand pounds of our own money and that we should also be allowed to take this out. I firmly disagreed and stated I would not go along with this. Perhaps the police side of me still believed that theft is theft and would not be happy to condone this. If I allowed Steve to do this, it would give a green light to go further, and I just did not want to go there.

I suggested to Steve we pay Mishare thirty thousand dollars this month, maybe fifty, but no more. I was to find out later he paid him seventy-five.

MISHARE BACKLASH

Back in the UK and after a catch-up with the kids and some sleep, I was back to interviewing. I really enjoyed interviewing, and at least now I could speak with some authority as this time I had actually walked the walk. A lot of the guys were from recommendations of those already with us. Also, many guys had just left the Army, having completed a tour in Iraq. The Royal Regiment of Wales had not long returned and were already warned off for another tour, so many resigned and were now looking to do the same sort of work but to get paid three to four times the amount in the private sector.

One afternoon, after completing some interviews, Steve called me and asked me to pop up to his house. I was rather surprised as he was supposed to be in Kuwait. When I arrived at his place, he proceeded to tell me about a meeting he had arranged in London but the guy he was due to meet could not make it as he had to attend a funeral. So Steve thought he would head home to Cardiff for a couple of days while he waited to hear from him again.

While at Steve's I took a call on my mobile from SO back in Kuwait. He wanted to know where Steve was. On explaining I was at Steve's house, SO stated he would call on the landline and suggested he be put on speakerphone.

'Mishare is extremely pissed off and wants to know why you are both out of country,' reported SO.

'Why, what's the matter?' asked Steve.

'Exactly that. Both of you are out of the country, and he is pissed off that he thinks we're not taking this seriously,' further explained SO.

I glared at Steve. He had intermitted that Mishare knew he was going to London for a meeting. Obviously not.

'In a nutshell, he has frozen the bank accounts and said if you are both not back within forty-eight hours he will close down the company,' explained SO.

'For fuck's sake,' I exclaimed. 'How serious is he?'

'I would guess fairly serious, as he says he has frozen the bank account, which he can do,' said SO.

We discussed the situation for a few minutes. 'Look, we still owe Mishare about three hundred and fifty grand for his loan,' I said, looking at Steve and raising my eyebrows. 'He is not going to close the company down. He is just giving our ears a little tweak to pull us into line. We can fly back out on Saturday and go and see him,' I suggested.

It was agreed that Steve and I would fly back on Saturday and then all three of us would go and see Mishare. It was Thursday, and I had been back in the UK for only just over a week. I was again pissed off with Steve for coming back to the UK. Now I would have to cut short my stay, and I still had interviews lined up, which I now had to cancel.

The following day Steve called and said Diane and he wanted to call around. When they turned up, Diane looked pale. She proceeded to explain that she had heard that in places like Kuwait, people were arrested for no apparent reason and thrown in prison for long periods.

'Steve, is there something I should know about?' I asked. My mind was racing to think of what Steve might have done to warrant Diane reacting like this. She was a smart woman, and obviously something had spooked her. After an hour of discussing it, we agreed Steve and I would still fly back the following day and would meet at Cardiff Train Station to catch the train to London.

'Mike, I am not going to make the flight back,' said Steve over the phone. I was in a taxi nearing the train station. 'I had a medical the other day, and I am still waiting for some results. Look, I don't want to go into detail, but it may be serious,' explained Steve.

'Oh, OK,' I said. 'Look, sort yourself out and let me know what happens.'

'Look, if there is any hint that you are going to get arrested, then get out of Kuwait, OK?' said Steve in a matter-of-fact way, as if he were giving advice about complaining about a meal I was not happy with.

I hung up the phone and thought, You spineless bastard. I recalled being told that Steve had a tendency to pull the medical card out whenever he was facing potential trouble. Often people would not question medical emergencies! And on this occasion, how could I, even though I was certain it was a load of bollocks? I was not really worried about Mishare's course of action. I guess I would do the same in his shoes, or rather sandals. But I did quickly have a vision of the prison in Midnight Express and me getting rogered by some Kuwaiti guards. I put the thought out of my head and boarded the train.

The following day, suited and booted, I headed for the Chamber of Commerce, where Mishare's office was located. SO had called to say he was tied up with embassy business so would not be able to make it. So I was to face the music on my own. Mishare was his usual charming self, immaculate in appearance and relaxed. I explained Steve's medical dilemma and hammed it up a little. As I had assessed, Mishare was not too upset. He had frozen the account but just wanted reassurance that in future either Steve or I would be in country and that we would agree on a repayment schedule for his loan. I diplomatically agreed, and all was well again.

'You must not always play the angel, Michael,' said Mishare with a slight grin on his face. I looked at him quizzically. 'In our faith we also have the angel Michael,' he said. I guessed he was making a religious comparison and simply smiled. I felt that in his own way he was telling me that he did not really think I was the problem but more so

Steve. Or was he trying to drive a wedge or test my loyalty to Steve? Despite Steve testing my patience, we had entered this together and must remain solid.

The following day I met up with SO. He had arranged a meeting with some guys from Bechtel at the SAS Radisson Hotel. Before the meeting, SO and me sat and had a coffee in the lounge and milled over the Mishare meeting. SO's assessment was the same as mine. Mishare was more concerned about Steve's actions than anything else.

As we walked a short distance to Bechtel's offices, SO stopped and said, 'Is Steve really the right guy to be promoting SFI?'

At first I did not know where SO was coming from. I gave him a puzzled look. He continued, 'Look, he's a big chap—well, fat—and does not really portray the right sort of image of an ex-military security company.'

'Agreed,' I said. 'But he is good at getting in front of people. If only he would then bow out and leave the ops planning to me.'

'I am sure you could do the initial work and we would not need him at all then,' replied SO as he appeared to be looking intently into my eyes, as if to be looking for a reaction. I now realised where this was heading but maintained my apparent ignorance as to what SO meant.

'I guess I could, but Steve would still want to be involved,' I said.

'I don't think we need him at all,' SO said in a blunt, matter-of-fact tone.

'Are you suggesting we push him out completely?' I asked with a slight scowl on my face.

'Why not? He is the wrong image and does not lend anything else to the party,' he replied.

'Listen, we all came into this together, and we see it through. I know Mishare is a little pissed at the moment, but that's sorted now,' I fired back. Despite Steve's annoying habits of heading back to the UK all the time, he was my mate, and without him we would not have got started. I was angered and quite frankly surprised that SO wanted to oust Steve. They had known each other longer than I had known Steve and could not believe that SO wanted to act like this.

'Now is as good a time as any. Mishare would back us. He knows that Steve is the problem and he would be more cooperative if Steve was sidelined. And quite frankly Steve does not appear to be fully committed to this. You went back on leave after an extended period out here and only a week later he headed back to UK. And Mishare was pissed at that', S O outlined as if presenting the case for the prosecution.

'No. We stick together', I replied and pulled open the office door and walked in.

SO followed as I heard him mutter, 'Oh well, it was an opportunity.'

The meeting with Bechtel was cordial but fruitless. I returned to the villa and pondered SO's stance. I decided to let it go and not mention anything to Steve. As long as we remained tight, it was OK.

As the summer progressed we picked up small contracts, and the Jap convoy kept rolling to Samawah. Also the invoices rolled out, and the cash rolled in. The repayment schedule we had agreed with Mishare was being met, and for now all was good in the garden.

CASUALTIES MOUNT

It was the first week of August, and Chris stormed into my office. 'We have a casualty,' he stuttered, out of breath, and ran back out towards the ops room. I quickly followed and started imagining the worst.

In the ops room, Dave was on the phone and giving out lots of 'eh, eh'. We all stared at him in anticipation. Eventually, he hung up, smiled, and said, 'All sorted.'

'Well?' I asked.

'OK, convoy returned from Samawah, and about twenty klicks south of Scannia one of the wagons veered off the road and rolled down the bank. Rob was thrown from the vehicle and appears to have a broken leg. Everyone else OK. Helicopter from multinational div en route,' Dave calmly explained.

'What, so an RTA then?' I asked.

'Yep, not sure why but think some debris in the road caused blowout and driver lost control,' Dave clarified.

'So not enemy action?' I asked rhetorically.

'And ironically, Rob is the team medic,' said Chris.

Within twenty minutes of the incident Rob was being loaded to a helicopter and taken to the military hospital at Shaibah Log Base. Our first casualty, and what was reassuring was the lines of communications we had established ensured that when we needed support, it was quick in coming.

Rob suffered a broken hip, leg, and ankle. I spent the next week coordinating with our insurance company to get Rob repatriated back to the UK. Thankfully, it was an injury he would recover from and again showed the system for repatriating injured men. I guessed, similar for bodies!

As a side note, he later went to Indonesia on holiday

for Christmas, and while relaxing on a beach on 26 December 2004 he had to beat a hasty retreat to avoid the tsunami that so devastated the region. Rob put his medical training to use and volunteered to stay and helped many of the victims for several months afterwards. Hats off to him. Good man.

I returned to the UK for a week and returned on the evening of 25 August. Steve, who was supposed to be in Kuwait for a further two weeks, met me at the airport. He was flying out, stating he had a meeting in London. He briefed me on what was going on and mentioned we had taken on a short-notice contract to recover some plant equipment from a construction site near Baghdad. It was for KBR, and he was excited that this could be our foot in the door. Chalky had departed that morning with a team and should have reached BIAP by nightfall.

By the time I reached the villa it was about 1:00 am. I quickly popped into the ops room to confirm the team had reached BIAP. With the knowledge they had, I retired to my pit.

The following morning I rose and was clearing some e-mails before getting some breakfast. Chris came in with a stern look on his face.

'We've had a contact, just South of Samara, one casualty, casevac requested,' he said.

Casevac stood for 'casualty evacuation' and could come in the form of road or air transport. We had good links with the US Military ops room in BIAP. Major Danny Sample was our man, and he was always very helpful. I made my way to the ops room.

'Rob Edwards is the casualty. Looks like a minor injury. Possible loss of just his thumb. Took a round to the hand,' reported Simon as I entered.

I took the sat phone and spoke to Chalky. 'What's the sitrep (situation report), Chalky?' I asked.

'Ambush from both sides of the road from elevated positions. Looks like they tried to disable lead vehicle by shooting engine block. They did destroy the engine, but we managed to nudge in behind it and push on through. We re-orged about three klicks down the road, and now heli casevac on site. Looks like Rob has taken a round to his right hand. None life-threatening,' reported Chalky in a calm, professional manner.

'Roger that. What is your intention now, to return to BIAP?' I asked.

'Ycp, will have to and will need replacement wagon, preferably two,' replied Chalky.

I asked Chris to brief me on the vehicles and crews deployed and was stunned to learn that there were only two vehicles and six men. Chris further explained that Steve had taken a job to escort trailers into a construction site in Baiji to recover some pieces of earth-moving plant for KBR. The site had been closed down as it was regularly mortared, and KBR wanted the plant out as they were paying a fortune in hire costs. He further explained that Steve had accepted extremely low rates, on the belief that if we took the job, we would get more from KBR. He had deployed only two vehicles and six men because he wanted to remain within budget. Now I understood why Steve had been vague the evening before at the airport. I was fuming.

I tried to call Steve, but he did not answer. I sent him an e-mail stating that in future if he wanted to deploy an under-strength team on a dangerous mission, he should stick around for the consequences. I awaited his reply.

I instructed Chris to look at deploying a further two vehicles and enough guys to make three per vehicle. Baiji was within the Sunni Triangle and would be a tough place to extract some large earth-moving plant. I also discussed with Chalky and insisted that if he believed it too risky, he was to abort.

I received a message back that Rob did not want his brother told about his injury. His brother Dai was also working with us and was in the villa right now. He was also likely to be one of the extra guys we were going to deploy, as we were running short. Despite Rob's request, I made the decision to inform Dai. It was inevitable that he was going to hear about it shortly, in any case. I also wanted to inform him now in the villa rather than have him find out while in an operational situation upcountry. I called him to my office and informed him. He was naturally worried about Rob, but I assured him that Rob was being well taken care of and was going to be flown to the military hospital in Germany. We would also arrange to try and get him to speak on the sat phone. I then discussed with Dai if he was good to still deploy. He assured me he was. Later that day he informed me he had spoken to Rob and that he was happy to deploy.

I began the process via the insurance company. They appointed an organisation called Specialty Assistance Services, who were to arrange the repatriation. They were excellent in this respect and quickly arranged the flight to Germany and the subsequent medical treatment. They kept me informed at all times and also assisted in sorting a replacement passport for Rob, as it had got lost.

After a couple of days I followed up on Rob's progress and learnt that he had lost most of his right hand. All that remained was his thumb. He had set up a fencing business after leaving the Army, and this was obviously going to be a problem.

Steve eventually replied in e-mail and stated that he had made the decision himself based on commercial reasons and considered the low price as a loss leader in order to try and gain future contracts with KBR. I explained that we were not Sainsbury's and we were not selling bloody golden delicious apples. I was more concerned about the risk to the guys, which appeared to escape him.

The reinforcements linked up with Chalky at BIAP, and the following day they continued on towards Baiji. They pulled into a small military base not too far from their intended destination. Following some discussion with the local US Military, Chalky decided to complete the extraction under cover of darkness the following night. All went well, and they managed to load the plant to the trailers without any unwanted interest. However, as they were preparing to depart, they came under mortar and small-arms fire. Executing a fighting withdrawal, Chalky and his team laid down covering fire while the trailers were driven as quickly as possible out and away from the location. Another job well done.

When the team returned to the villa, the vehicle in which Rob was in was inspected. From what we worked out the round that hit him had come through the left rear of the vehicle, through his headrest, and as it exited the vehicle through the open front passenger window it struck Rob's right hand. He had been firing an MP5K, and in order to get a rearward shot he had leant forward against the dash, with his right arm outstretched out through the door window. Had Rob not been leant forward, the round would have caught him in the back of the head and almost certainly have killed him. The round had struck his hand on the opposite side to his thumb and then traversed through his flanges. The MP5K had been on a lanyard attached to Rob, so although he let go of the weapon it was retained. We followed through with our theory and examined the MP5K. It was covered in Rob's blood, and we could see the plastic cover of the pistol grip had been damaged, and there was a small hole in the one side. On shacking the weapon there was something rattling inside it. I used my Leatherman and opened up the pistol grip, and there inside was the head of the round. Dai was with me when I got it out. I gave it to him to keep for Rob. I heard later he made it into a pendant.

Over the next few weeks I argued with the insurance company regarding compensation payout for Rob. They had covered the repatriation and medical costs. But I was now chasing the compensation, which I believed Rob was entitled to. They argued that partial loss of a hand did not come under the definition of 'loss of limb', which under their small print did not. However, having trawled the small print I found a clause that stated that if the insured could no longer perform gainful employment for which they 'had been trained or experience in', then they would get full payout. When I argued that Rob was trained and experienced as an infantry soldier and, since leaving the Army, was experienced in fencing—both of these forms of gainful employment he could no longer do—they paid out.

Through our work with the Jap convoys to Samawah I had formed a relationship with some of the guys with the Japanese International Cooperation Society (JICS). Their role was to foster business interests on behalf of the Japanese government. As they were not allowed into Iraq, they used their British counterpart, Crown Agents. From this relationship SFI was asked to bid to take into Iraq thirty fire engines which were being donated to the Iraqi people by the Japanese. We had several meeting with the Japanese defence attaché, which SO facilitated. I also flew to Jordan for a meeting with the Japanese ambassador and JICS at the Japanese embassy in Amman. Some of the fire engines were to be taken in through Basra and some though Jordan. More meetings were to follow.

THE CIA

In late September I was in my office when I heard the front doorbell ring. On answering, I found two men dressed in dark suits and wearing dark sunglasses.

'Hello, Securiforce International?' asked one of them in an American accent.

'Yes, it is. And can I ask who you are?' I responded.

'May we come in to discuss some potential business?' the second asked.

'Of course, come in,' I replied and led them into my office. 'Can I offer you some coffee or anything to drink?' I offered. They declined.

'What sort of business are you in, and what can SFI offer you?' I asked.

'We're more interested in your facilities here at your villa' came the reply, which took me a little bit by surprise. I paused to ponder the situation. Here were two Americans in dark suits, who appear to not want to answer any questions I put to them and were interested in our villa. Competitors assessing our setup? I thought.

'Here is my business card,' I said, handing each one. The normal custom would be to exchange cards. None were forthcoming. 'Do you have cards?' I enquired.

'Would it be possible to have a look around?' one asked, ignoring my request for a card. Both had not yet cracked a smile and, quite frankly, were starting to piss me off.

'MIB?' I asked with a smirk on my face. I decided that if they were going to be awkward, then so would I. A measure of sarcasm was needed.

'Excuse me?' one asked with a puzzled look on his face.

'Men in Black,' I replied. 'The dark suits, shades. Which one of you has that neuraliser thing that will make me forget all about your visit there?' I continued, taking the piss out of the situation. I wanted to get some response to establish who they were or if I should just kick them out.

'Oh, very funny. I get it,' said one with a smile on his face. At last, some human emotion. With that, Simon knocked and walked in.

'Sorry, didn't realise you had company,' he said.

'It's OK, this is Agent Smith and Agent Smith from the CIA. They have come here to see if they can rent a bed,' I said, still trying to invoke a reaction. Simon immediately sensed from my tone that I was taking the piss but was also mildly irritated with these two guys.

'Oh, I thought they were MIB. You know ...'

'Yes, we know, Men in Black,' interrupted one. I thought they are starting to get the picture. Simon left the room.

'OK, guys, this has been a breeze, but I have work to do. So unless you want to tell me who you are and what exactly you want, then I am afraid I need you to leave,' I said as I rose to my feet and indicated towards the door with my arm.

'OK, we are from the CIA, and we are interested in using your villa as a safe house,' said one of the guys in a very matter-of-fact manner.

'Yeah, right' was my immediate reply, still moving towards the door.

Referring to a small notebook one of them rattled off, 'Securiforce International is a private security company specialising in convoy mitigation in Iraq. Mostly former British Military, you use this villa as your base. There are four partners, with Mishare Al Ghazali as your Kuwaiti sponsor.' This info was easily available, I thought. 'Over the past few weeks you have had several visitors, including the

British defence attaché, the Japanese defence attaché, members of JICS, and Crown Agents. We have been watching,' he concluded and put away his notebook. They clearly had been watching us.

Sitting back down I asked, 'OK, so let's take it that you are in fact from the CIA. What do you want from us?'

'Like I said, we are interested in your facility here,' he said. He went on to explain that with the Iraqi elections due, there would be numerous UN observers deployed and they would initially come to Kuwait for briefing before deploying to Iraq. They were looking for suitable places to take these delegates in the event of an incident. I explained we could sleep up to seventy people and could also provide catering. They stated that our villa was one of several locations they were assessing and that it would be essential that this be kept confidential, to which I agreed.

'So, we will be in touch if we are going to take this further,' they said as they were leaving.

'So which one of you is Mr Smith?' I joked as they left. Neither cracked a smile.

We never heard from them again, and as there were no incidents to my knowledge, then I guessed a safe house was not needed. However, what it did highlight for me was that if they had been watching us as closely as it appeared, they must have seen the weapons being carried to and from the vehicles at the rear yard? If this was the case, would they report this? If they had seen it, could other authorities have been watching us? We needed to get our weapons out from Kuwait and set up in Iraq.

THE V94 TURBINE RECCE

In October 2004 I made a trip to Abu Dhabi to discuss with ALE possible movement of a large V94 turbine generator from Jordan to Kirkuk. The route was uncertain, and the project was being run by Siemens Westinghouse, based out of Tampa, Florida. The problem was that their security provider was a company called Britam, and James has been out on part of the route survey and was not impressed. He reported that all they had were beaten-up old cars, and their preferred MO was to blend in rather than present an overt security presence. This was fine for movement of people, but for a large slow-moving convoy, ALE wanted SFI.

ALE's GM, John Ruston, was due to go to Tampa to present a solution. The solution had not yet been found, but most of the route had been surveyed and was OK. However, there was about 200 kilometres of what was reportedly an old smuggler's route that ran in a southeasterly direction from the Syrian border towards Baghdad. Britam had stated it was too dangerous, as that area was rife with insurgency activity and that the route probably was unsuitable for heavy-haul transport. They were probably right, but there was only one way to find out. A route survey would take place, with SFI taking James Roberts to look for this desert track.

A week later, James flew to Kuwait, and a team was assembled. The day before departure, there was a distinct different atmosphere in the villa. There had been discussions about this smuggler's route, and I sensed some apprehension amongst the ranks. The TL (team leader), Paul, was ex-para reg and a good medic. There were more than the usual briefings about anti-ambush drills. The night before, Paul came to see me and expressed his concerns that the team would be pretty exposed in the area the route survey would take place. We discussed that, in open desert, with good fields of view, it should not be a problem, but the move into and out from this open desert area took you through small villages and lots of potential for attack.

Early the following morning and still in darkness, the team departed the villa.

'Stay low, move fast, trust no one,' I said to James as they headed out.

I was due to fly to Jordan early the following morning for a meeting for a future job, and to be honest, I was thankful that I had to, as otherwise I would probably have led the mission myself due to the nature. But we now had good TLs, and I believed the guys preferred to operate without one of the company directors dipping in and out. I felt bad as I had sensed the apprehension of the guys, but we also needed to bring other business.

Just after lunch we received a call from the team. They had crossed over the border into Iraq and were heading along route Tamper when a local Iraqi pickup had driven at right angles into the path of the lead vehicle and was T-boned. At first it was believed to be a suicide bomber, but quickly the guys realised it was an accident. At that point route Tamper was a dust track, and in the thick dust the locals had not seen our guys. Sadly one of the locals was killed instantly by the impact and another seriously injured. The guys rendered first aid and arrange helicopter medical evacuation via the local Multinational Force, whose area it was in.

The result was that one of our vehicles was written off, but thankfully no injuries to our guys. But it did mean the mission could not carry on, and so they cross-loaded all equipment into the remaining two vehicles and headed back. By early evening they arrived at the villa. I called in Paul, and we discussed prepping another vehicle and heading out the following day. We were now up against a time factor, as John Ruston was due to walk into a meeting in Tampa and needed to say that we had established a viable route. If we could not, then we would not get the contract. If we could, then ALE and SFI would be in.

After Paul and I finished discussing the incident, he walked out of my office and about five minutes later returned.

'I don't think I will be able to go on this job. I think I have food poisoning and don't feel too good,' he said. I looked at Paul, and he was avoiding eye contact.

'When did this start?' I asked.

'I didn't feel too good this morning. Must have been some dodgy eggs or something,' he replied, still avoiding eye contact.

I sensed this was not the real reason. 'Look, I appreciate that it has not been a good start to the mission, but you have a good team with lots of experience. As long as everyone stays alert and no undue risks are taken, there should not be a problem,' I said.

'Yeah, I know, but ...' Paul stuttered.

'You're a medic, what do you think? Are you fit to deploy or not?' I asked in a bit more of a blunt manner.

With his head now slightly lowered and still avoiding eye contact, he confirmed he was not fit to deploy.

I called in Pete, who was another TL and ex-commando artillery. I spend about twenty minutes briefing him on the mission, and after I had finished, he said, 'I will go on the job as a shooter, but I won't lead it.'

I was taken aback by this as Pete had been a warrant officer, and I was surprised at his reluctance to lead. He got up and left. Shortly after, James came in.

'Listen, mate, far be it from me to tell you how to run your company, but the guys are scared. I can see it in their eyes,' he said. 'They need strong leadership, and you need to take this one.'

'I have to go to Jordan tomorrow, and it shouldn't need me to lead this thing,' I replied.

James then went down on to his knees, looked up at me, and said, 'I am begging you to lead this one.'

I placed my hand on his head and moved my crotch towards his face. 'While you're down there,' I joked.

The humour quickly vanished as James maintained a stern look on his face. I realised he was deadly serious. For a few seconds, I thought 'Holy shit, this is a dangerous mission, and I don't want to go on it.' But this is where leadership comes into its own. I was flattered that James had deemed my leadership pivotal and also that I simply could not make anyone take this role if I were not prepared to do so myself.

'OK. Let me make some calls and see if I can rearrange the meeting,' I said as James got up from his embarrassing position. I made some calls and was able to push back the meetings I had planned. Something in my head was telling me this was a wrong move. After a quick briefing, plans were put in place to depart early the next morning. I turned in to bed and took a while to drift off as I considered whether the recce should go ahead. I do not believe in omens, but the universe appeared to be talking to me and I was choosing not to listen. There was certainly an element that I felt I could not call it off now that I was involved. That would have looked bad, and at the end of the day no other further information had come to light regarding the recce that changed the mission.

After the now-customary farewell of 'stay low, move fast, trust no one' from Shep, we departed. But this time it seemed more pertinent. James had tried to re-establish contact with Ali from the Ministry of Electricity but could not raise him. He was given another number and had made contact and tried to agree an RV. They appeared nervous and reluctant to meet anywhere populated. James and I discussed this, and I suggested we met somewhere we could observe them and then tell them to move to another location. This way, if there was something untoward or they were followed, we may have a chance of seeing other movement. We agreed to meet under the steel bridge in Ramadi just outside a US Army base at 0900 hrs the following day.

Early the next morning we were up and out of BIAP, heading for the US base in Ramadi. The US Marines were still there, and we reported into their ops cell to advise of our intended movements that day and to glean any intel for the area we were to move through. Having been advised there was little activity in the area, we headed for the gate, where we could observe the RV point.

Right on time we saw a grey 4×4 pull up, and we saw two men get out. James called the number given, and we could see one of them raise a mobile to his ear. James explained that we had moved on and were waiting just off the road at the start of the desert track and asked them to make their way there. He agreed, and we saw them get in and head off. Seeing no other movement, we headed off and followed along a raised single-track tarmac road which wound its way northwest from Ramadi to the north of the River Euphrates for about 25 kilometres. We kept the 4×4 in sight but did not close on it. As it pulled off the tarmac road onto the track, we closed rapidly. The two guys jumped out and cowered behind their vehicle. We all dismounted and took up positions. Then a young man appeared from behind the vehicle, and I heard him say, 'Mr Mike, good to see you again.' He moved towards me, and then I recognised him as Yousif, Ali's young apprentice. He was evidently glad to see me, and I him. He explained that it was not good to be seen with Westerners and was also nervous as to who he would be meeting up with.

Yousif explained that he had been told that Ali had died a few weeks ago from a heart attack. This was sad to hear, as I had grown fond of Ali; he was one of the good guys.

So there we were. About 150 kilometres of desert track to navigate and GPS-record the route and assess its viability to take a heavy-lift trailer and cargo over. We also had to reach the end, make a conclusion, and inform John before he stepped into the meeting in Tampa. We had until 1400 hrs local time to make the call. In any case, I wanted to get it over and done with early so we had time to make it back to BIAP before darkness.

We headed off. I informed the lead vehicles to follow Yousif and only slow down if James wanted to look at anything. The rest of the guys were told to keep their eyes peeled. This was an old smuggler's route from Syria to Baghdad and reportedly used by the insurgency. I did not want any unexpected encounters. As we progressed, there was a clear track, and we maintained a reasonable speed. Our fields of view were good, and apart from a few areas we could see for quite some distance. James reported that a few places would require some civil works, but with a grader leading the convoy it would be navigable by the trailer.

We reached the tarmac road running northeast from Hadidah to Baiji. With about five minutes to spare, James called John on the sat phone and reported a viable route. John was literally standing outside the meeting room in Tampa, waiting for the news. So far, so good.

Yousif stated he and his colleague would leave us and head for Baiji. We had taken nearly four hours to complete the desert track and would not have had enough time to return the same way. We had planned to cross the Euphrates at Hadidah and take an oil pipeline road southeast back to join Highway 1 just west of Ramadi. This should take us about two hours and back to BIAP in good time. From our briefing at the marines' base, the route was good, and little activity was reported.

About twenty minutes later we reached the bridge over the Euphrates. However, the bridge was no longer there. Instead, a makeshift pontoon bridge was in its place. On the home bank there was a small village and a larger built-up area on the far bank. The crossing was about 150 metres, and I could only see foot passage being made across. I had three vehicles and nine of us armed. Our main concern was, of course, James. He was our client. I did not want to stay where we were for too long. Locals were paying too much interest in us, and I could see several with mobile phones to their ears. Word was being spread.

I gathered the guys in for a snap briefing. We were to dismount vehicles and get a team of three men across to the far bank on foot as quickly as possible. Then, with a firm fire base on each bank, the vehicles would move one at a time across the floating bridge. Speed was of the essence as we were spread thin and vulnerable as the vehicles crossed. I was concerned not only about the potential threat from small-arms fire but also the integrity of the bridge.

Pete and two others ran across the bridge and took up positions on the far side. The positions were not great tactical positions, and the exit route ran up from the river and gave very little fields of view. But their best view was back to our side and along the riverbank either side of us. Likewise, we could observe their side better from where we were.

The impending feeling of doom returned. Again I questioned myself and the decision to go ahead rather than turn back. From arriving at the crossing, it had only been a few minutes. Could the bad guys mount something that fast? If they were to mount an attack, the longer we took, the more likely they would.

'Go, go, go,' I urged as the first wagon started to cross. The intention was that as soon as it reached the far bank and cleared the bridge, the second wagon would start. As the pontoons took the weight of the vehicle, there was little movement, and it appeared quite sturdy. I felt a little better.

'Shit, we got a blowout,' I heard over the radio. As the first wagon was about to clear the bridge, it caught a jagged piece of steel that tore the wall of the rear right-side tyre. I then heard the roar of the engine as it climbed up the embankment with the wheel spinning and the tyre shredding. Fuck, I thought. I have the team split either side of the river, and now a disabled vehicle. We all had to get to the other side as quickly as possible. I looked over to John Fisher in the second wagon. 'OK, go, steady, but don't hang around.'

'Roger that, Boss,' replied John, and off he went.

'Vehicle approaching at speed, far bank, from north' came over the radio. I looked and could see a pickup heading along the road towards the exit point. It was travelling fast, but through the treeline I could not make out if there was anyone in the back or see any weapons. 'John, keep going, everyone else, stand to,' I snapped over the radio. My heart was in my mouth. The guys were all in fire positions, and John was steadily making his way across. 'It's going straight past, no worries' came over the radio. Up until now I had not paid too much attention to the far side beyond the treeline. Now I could see quite a lot of vehicular movement and could make out what appeared to be a line of buildings, possibly shops. The exit from the bridge was into the centre of a small village. Not surprising, really, as it would be a logical place for a village to be.

The sense of urgency then got the better of me. John had reached about three-quarters of the way across in the second wagon. 'OK, let's go,' I said to Rob, who was the driver of the final wagon. Rob pulled forward. 'James, with me,' I called. As the third wagon moved across the bridge, the remainder of us started to move on foot behind it.

'As soon as Bravo clears the river, all-round defence, and get the tyre changed on Foxtrot,' I called over the radio. The guys were already ahead, and as Rob pulled the last wagon clear of the bridge the jack was already under and the flat tyre was off. There was a short dog-leg leading up onto the main road. Some of the guys moved forward to get onto some higher ground. Once again tyre-changing drills paid off, as in only a few minutes Foxtrot was good to go.

'OK, mount up, formation, let's go,' I said with some relief. As we headed off it was apparent that it was a busy little place, with what appeared to be a small marketplace.

We headed south for about 5 kilometres and then picked up the oil pipeline road. This ran dead straight southeast towards Ramadi, running parallel to a series of villages and small towns between this road and the Euphrates. We picked up speed as the road undulated before us. After about 30 kilometres we came over the brow of a hill to find the road blocked with US Military vehicles. As we came to a rapid stop there was a flurry of activity from the military. Foxtrot came to a stop and displayed the Union Jack. Thankfully, they realised who we were, and all was calmed. One of them explained that the road further ahead was mined and we would have to divert back onto the road running down through the villages and towns. We had about three hours of daylight left and would need all of that to reach BIAP. We diverted off the pipeline road and carried on.

The road had buildings scattered along its route. There was traffic on the road, and every now and again there was a police vehicle parked to the side of the road. Ever policeman we passed was on his mobile. My spider senses started to tingle again. 'Anyone else spotted the interest from the police?' I asked.

'We're definitely being dicked,' replied Rob from the rear vehicle.

I was scanning the map to see if we could cut back across on to the pipeline road. I assessed we had cleared the mined area, and on that road it was straight and out in the open. On the road we were on, there were built-up areas, lots of vegetation to the sides, and far too much interest in our movement from the local constabulary.

As we approached the small town called Hit I could see there was a chance to divert back towards the pipeline road. As we entered the town there was a roundabout, with what appeared to be a monument in the middle of it. As Foxtrot rounded it and we started to enter the roundabout, I caught a glance of the main street ahead. It was completely empty. All our windows were down and barrels pointing out, as was the drill in built up-areas like this. My spider senses were now screaming at me, and I was about to talk over the radio when I heard a few pops. Immediately I saw the barrels of the lead vehicle extend outwards and muzzle flash.

'Contact, contact' squawked over the radio. At this point we were now midway around the roundabout. Foxtrot was exiting the roundabout and entering the main street through Hit. I could see for several hundred metres in a straight line. The road was a double-lane road with what appeared to be about 20 metres either side of the road as forecourts to buildings running the length of the main street. The buildings were set back, double story, made of breeze-block construction. Most had openings where windows should have been. They appeared to run the length of the main street, providing a real rat run and an ideal ambush site.

A movement to my right caught my eye. I looked along the edge of the line of the building and saw a figure emerging from a doorway with what appeared to be a long pipe, and it was being raised above the shoulder. Shit, RPG, I thought and immediately loosed of a couple of rounds in his direction. I had only a split second and lost sight as we entered the rat run. By now I could hear rounds going off from all around me. I looked up at a second-floor window to see muzzle flash from the darkness. I fired a short burst and could see a few puffs of dust jump out as my rounds hit the breeze block around the window opening. I was firing an MP5 and knew the rounds would not penetrate. But it may deter the other guy from taking aimed shots.

Over the radio I could hear multiple reports of contacts from right side, left side, on top of the buildings, and from the rear. As John accelerated our wagon we closed rapidly on Foxtrot. Pete had panicked and had knocked the gearstick forward, expecting to change down a gear so as to accelerate, forgetting it was automatic. The vehicle, now being in neutral, slowed. 'Put the vehicle in drive and go,' said John in a calm but firm voice over the radio. This was the experience of a driver who knew what he was doing. Foxtrot accelerated, and so did we. I again scanned the buildings and could now see muzzle flash from many windows. The tarmac around our vehicle was spitting up gravel as the rounds thumped into the ground. I could hear the distinctive sound of the SLR and found comfort from the fact that the 7.62 millimetre rounds could well be going through the breeze block. 'Changing mag' I could hear being shouted out. Training says that we should count our rounds. Fuck that. I just kept firing bursts at every muzzle flash I could see. When my weapon stopped firing, I changed my mag.

We were about halfway along the main street. From a doorway to our right I saw a man stand from a crouching position and raise an AK. The curved mag gave it away. As he levelled the weapon I fired a burst. As we sped past I just saw the weapon drop as he slumped backwards, out of sight into the doorway.

We accelerated on, and I could hear small explosions

from the rear as Bravo threw small Chinese grenades.

I then felt a sharp stinging sensation in the back of my neck. I froze for a split second and turned my head to my left. I could see John with the MP5K machine pistol firing up to his left with one hand and holding the radio in his other, shouting for Foxtrot to accelerate. Feeling no further sensation, I assumed I was OK and turned again to my right. We were just clearing the end of the building and about to exit the town. We were travelling quite fast now. The last thing we needed was for a vehicle to lose control and spin off.

With all the chaos going off around, I actually felt very calm. I had not been in such an intense situation before, and I had imagined how I would react. I was the leader, and I needed to keep control of what was going on.

'Bravo, all OK back there? Any casualties, any damage?' I asked.

'Negative' came the reply.

'Foxtrot, casualties, damage?' I repeated.

'That's a negative' thankfully came the reply.

I was conscious that I could no longer hear gunfire and only road noise. I glanced at the speedo, and we were doing nearly 200 kilometres per hour. Speed was a good ally, but too much was not.

'OK, let's slow it down but keep moving. Pete, bring it down to 120,' I ordered to Foxtrot.

The road heading away from the town was a slow sweeping right-hand bend. About 500 metres ahead I could see blue shirts of police out on the road with a line of civilian traffic behind them. The bastards had stopped traffic coming into the ambush area. The bastards had set it up. My immediate thought was to let them have half a mag as we sped by. I then quickly assessed that if I was thinking that, the guys would likely be thinking the same.

'OK, nobody shoots at the police,' I shouted over the

radio.

As we passed, the scowls on their faces could be clearly seen.

We were in the clear, but I was conscious that we may have sustained damage to the vehicles. A shot brake line?

'OK, we will pull over in one klick and check over vehicles. All-round defence, drivers complete checks,' I said.

A little further on, Pete slowed and we all pulled over. The guys all jumped out, and there was obvious jubilation mixed with a huge amount of bravado.

'Did you see the one on the roof?' I heard someone say.

'I think I dropped a few,' said someone else. No one was taking up fire positions.

'Guys, we're not home and dry yet. All-round defence, and keep switched on. Sort the drills. Re-org, check ammo, vehicles. Come on, sort it out,' I snapped at them.

The adrenaline was still pumping, but I was trying to override it and remain calm and in control. As the vehicles were being checked over, I noticed a tickling sensation on my neck. I raised my hand to touch the back of my neck and could feel moisture. I lowered my hand to see it covered with blood. I froze. Was this one of these situations where I had been shot but through shock I did not realise? I felt OK. I didn't feel faint. I again raised my hand to check again. This time I could feel the sting of a cut and also something harder. I picked out from my collar a small piece of glass. I looked back at my vehicle and could see that the passenger door window behind my seat had been shot out. That was what the sharp stinging sensation I had felt during the ambush. Sandy explained that when the shooting had started he had grabbed James and forced him down into the foot well and placed spare body armour on top of him. Just as well, as a round had either entered or exited through James's closed window, shattering it and scattered glass, some of which had stuck my neck. I had blood drawn in enemy action. Perhaps I could now get a Purple Heart?

'Boss, over there,' said one of the guys, pointing. About a hundred metres away off the road were two US Military Humvees. They were stationary in a slight depression in the ground. I made my way over, and as I approached there were about six of them all huddled together, looking over a map. I approached with caution, as none of them had noticed an armed man approach them. I did not want to spook them.

'Good afternoon,' I said in a clear English accent. I stood with my weapon slung and both my arms out to the side. I could see they were startled but did not overreact, thankfully. I could see a set of sergeant's stripes and assumed he was their section leader.

'Hi, we're a private security team and just had a bit of a dust-up in Hit, and we almost certainly have left some dead. Not ours, but some of them,' I announced.

For what seemed like a long time they all just stood there looking at me.

'Just thought I would report it, in case you guys need to take any details?' I asked.

They continued to stare.

'We're all OK, and we're just checking our vehicles over,' I continued, in the hope of getting some sort of reaction.

'What the hell were you doing in there?' asked the sergeant, pointing back towards Hit.

'We were returning from a route survey and cleared it through your HQ this morning,' I replied with some curiosity.

'We had three platoons pinned down in there a couple of days back and had to call in air support to extract them. It's pretty much a no-go zone for military,' replied the sergeant.

'For fuck's sake!' I exclaimed. 'We got an area brief from your HQ this morning, and they said nothing much happens out here,' I continued.

'I'm really sorry, but it's kind of rough in there. You guys need any assistance?' asked the sergeant in an almost apologetic tone.

'No, we're good, thanks. We're gonna head on down to the highway and back into BIAP, so we'd better get going,' I replied and headed back to the roadside.

Upon returning to the vehicles and being assured all was well, we mounted up and headed off. There was very little talking the rest of the way back. I guessed all were reflecting on how lucky we were to have come out from Hit with little other than a few holes in our vehicles and a smashed window. Apart from a slight cut to my neck, there were no injuries.

As we pulled into BIAP I instructed over the radios to head for the DEFAC for some food and then to meet at 2000 hrs for a debrief.

As we walked towards the cookhouse I was thinking how James was feeling. He was a civvie and would not have even trained for such an event. 'How you feeling, mate? If you want to talk about it, then I'm ready to listen,' I asked.

'I'm fine. As it was happening, I was thinking how I was going to explain to your family that I begged you to come on this if you had been killed or seriously injured,' James explained as we walked. I was touched as the sincerity in which he said that was a measure of the man.

'And then I felt very frustrated that I didn't have a gun to shoot back,' James said.

Sensing that James was fine, I replied, 'You were sat immediately behind me. Do you really think I was going to give you a loaded weapon?' I slapping him on the back as we entered the cookhouse.

Later at the debrief it appeared that there was

anything between twenty to thirty insurgents involved in the ambush. There were positioned mostly in the windows of the first floor and some on the roof. The guy I spotted with the RPG was seen by the rear vehicle, scurrying back through a door. From various accounts it is possible that we got five or six of them.

I am certain that their intention was to fire the RPG from our rear, as a vehicle heading away is effectively a stationary target only getting smaller, whereas a side shot is at a moving target. But with the weight of fire that was returned, he headed back, and by the time he came back out we were well gone. I had established the drill that I called the Porcupine Effect, whereby when shots were fired at us, all were to return fire. If a target could be seen, then you shot at it. Otherwise, you took aimed shots into the ground in a safe place. The plan was to return a mass of fire with the intent of making the bad guys perhaps go from aimed shots to cowering behind cover and then to allow our speed to put distance between us. On our first test, I believe it proved effective, considering it was an ideal ambush setup and we should have been cut to ribbons. Chilling thought.

The attack in Hit appeared to be a turning point, as incidents began to be a matter of routine. Almost every convoy that we deployed on, there was an incident, ranging from a few random small-arms shots to more sustained shooting, to near misses with roadside IEDs.

Following a meeting with some of the guys, we decided to up-armour our vehicles. Most were still against going to fully B6 armoured vehicles, but we were to put in some steel plate to afford some protection. Another decision was to provide a better weapons platform for the V96 convoy as we wanted to really display an overt armed presence. We purchased some double-axle GMC pickups and built a steel plate box in the back to mount some machine guns. We had a mixture of GPMG (general-purpose machine guns), familiar to the guys as used by the British Military, and some RPKs, the Kalashnikov equivalent. One of our armourers rigged up a frame that mounted two RPKs side by side, each with a seventy-round drum mag. We had the GMCs painted with matt black IR-reflective paint for the price of some bottles of whiskey at the US base in Kuwait. These would provide a firm fire base for convoys and be located at the rear of the convoys. The net result was a mean-looking setup: the gun trucks.

It was not long before the gun trucks proved their worth. A convoy was delivering cargo to a small town called Mandelhay near the Iranian border northeast of Baghdad. As it was approximately 20 kilometres from its destination when the rear of the convoy was attached. This was the normal drill by the insurgents, as it was assessed the bad guys would not want the convoy still coming at them, rather attack from the rear and see what they could pick off. On this occasion there were approximately ten to fifteen insurgents along a grass line between two palm trees situated about 50 metres apart. The tail gunner in the gun truck was an ex–US Marine Corps guy called Andy. He swung the RPK pair around and loosed off both mags along the grass line. Some of the barrels protruding from the grass line dropped, and at least two heads were seen to slump down. The convoy continued unscathed.

As we came into the last quarter of 2004 we were looking quite good commercially. We had paid all of Mishare's loan back and with a team of forty-four guys on standby for the V94. We were billing at a standby rate of $600 per man per day, and when a team went into Iraq this increased to $1,150 per man per day. We were using the guys for other jobs, taking the risk that they would not be called forward for the V94 move. We had a contract in place, but a start date kept slipping. We had been picking up a few smaller contracts which all added to the bottom line, and we were comfortably covering our costs.

Steve announced he has secured another contract to provide armed guards for the rubbish trucks servicing the various British Military bases dotted around Basra and Alamara. Great, I thought, until he went into detail. We were to place one armed guard in the cab of the truck and were going to bill out at $400 per man per day. I blinked hard and stared at Steve in disbelief.

'Are you serious?' I asked.

'It's a high-volume contract, and the turnover will be big,' he explained with an element of self-contentment.

'It may be high turnover, but it's also going to be high costs with net profit in the negative. Come on, you must be winding me up,' I said hopefully.

'Why, it's a loss leader 'cos we will gain more contracts from this,' he explained.

'For fuck's sake, Steve, we are not Sainsbury's, selling golden delicious. This is men's lives at risk here,' I said with raised voice, realising he was serious. 'So how do we turn a profit on this when we pay the guys $350 per day and we still need cover all other costs?' I asked.

'We can clear about a million per annum,' he declared.

'OK, Steve, you go and write this all down and show me how you expect to achieve that,' I said to Steve, pointing towards his office. 'And I will also work out what I think it will be, and we can compare notes.'

Steve stormed off to his office. I opened up a spreadsheet I used for costing jobs. I had listed all the costs and filled in the numbers of guards needed and the rate Steve had agreed. The net result was a loss of just short of $1.5 million over a year. Steve came back out with not even a full piece of A4 paper; it was a torn-off piece which basically added the billing rate and deducted the guys' salaries. He concluded a $1 million profit.

'Steve, we have discussed this before that the salaries are about a third of our costs. You haven't allowed for any other costs in that for flights, insurance, weapons, ammunition, body armour, villa, ops room staff overheads, etc., etc.,' I said.

After about five minutes of a heated argument Steve stormed off to his room and never mentioned that job again. What it did clearly show was that Steve was approaching his business development duties as he did with most things — blag it and hopefully it will all work out.

Shortly after, Diane, his wife, came out to Kuwait to look over the books. She concluded that the accounts were in order and well run. I was pleased as it was turning into quite a monster, and we discussed taking on an accountant full time.

Diane expressed her concerns that Steve appeared anxious. 'He seems obsessed with trying to earn as much as me,' explained Diane. Steve had always bragged how she was on a six-figure salary with good quarterly bonuses. The way he was trying to cost jobs was not going to achieve that, I thought.

The conversation with SO about sidelining Steve came into mind, and perhaps it was not such a bad idea. Steve was spending less and less time in Kuwait and kept saying he had meetings in London but never produced anything from all these meetings. It became a bit of a joke in the ops room, with guys having a sweepstake on what excuse Steve would come up with when he was due to fly back out.

The fact remained that we had come into this as partners and Steve was an old mate and we would not have got off the ground without him. I was learning a lot about the business world and realised that sometimes you have to cut corners, but logical costing still had to come into it. I was starting to enjoy the business development side, and with the occasional trip up country as a shooter on a team when we were short, I was getting the best of both worlds. As long as Steve did not do anything too stupid or commit us to anything we could not do, then I was happy for him to take a lower profile.

Late in November of 2004 a convoy was returning with empty trailers towards BIAP when an IED detonated as one of our wagons went past. The blast spun the vehicle around, and it slammed into a crash barrier on the side of the road and burst into flames. An RPG was then fired at the vehicle and pierced through the lower part of the left-side rear passenger door. The warhead did not detonate but did impact into the lower left leg of Greg Cannons, who was sat in the rear. Greg tried to open the door, but the door was jammed from the impact. He managed to pull himself out through the door window. As he fell to the ground he could see the tail of the RPG still fizzing. At the same time Greg was extracting himself from the vehicle, the front-seat passenger, Andy Hinson, got out of the vehicle and ran to the driver's door. Mick Abraham was sat at the wheel and was on fire. Andy reached in and physically dragged Mick out through the door window and, using his jacket, managed to douse the flames.

As all this was going on there were small-arms fire incoming. The rest of the team repelled the remaining attackers and requested medical evacuation via the ops room.

Andy helped Greg and Mick away from the burning vehicle, and a short time later the warhead of the RPG detonated.

Again the response from US Military was rapid, and Greg and Mick were airlifted to medical facilities in BIAP. Mick suffered second-degree burns over 60 per cent of his body, and Greg lost the lower part of his left leg, below the knee.

As preparations were underway for the V94 convoy,

there was a lot of civil works needed to reinstate part of the route that was washed out in some recent rains. A civil contractor had been appointed by Siemens, but they wanted the progress of this work to be monitored. The US Military declined to do this, and SFI were asked to send a team to evaluate. We were on the dollar so could hardly refuse. The team visited the location and reported that work was about 50 per cent complete. On returning, the team were caught in a roadside IED, and one of the vehicles was written off. Thankfully, there were only a few minor cuts and bruises. The steel plate added to the vehicles was proving quite effective protection.

A few days later SFI was asked again to check another part of the route. Again while returning, there was an attack. As they travelled along Highway 1, running to the north of Ramadi, a civilian car packed with explosives pulled alongside the rear gun truck and detonated. All that was left of the suicide bomber's vehicle was the front axle, with bits of him and his car all over the road. The rest of the team closed in on the gun truck, fearing the worst due to the size of the explosion. It was stationary and totally peppered with shrapnel holes. 'We're OK, we're alive' came the report over the radio from Zippy (Richard Platt), who was inside the gun truck. Miraculously, all three guys were unharmed, apart from a perforated eardrum. The gun truck was a write-off.

On 5 January 2005 a convoy of twelve trailers with three of our security vehicles were travelling along Route Irish towards BIAP. In the lead vehicle was Rob Jones, driving, and Aled Owen in the front passenger seat. A roadside IED detonated to the left side of the vehicle. A length of rubber seal around the window lashed across Rob's face. He felt the immediate impact and pain and raised his hand to his face. He could feel something in the palm of his hand and realised it was his left eye. His first instinct was to slam on the brakes, but incredibly he remembered the drill to keep the convoy moving if the vehicle was not disabled. The windscreen was shattered, apart from a small section in the lower centre. He leaned down and to his right so he could see out of this one piece of clear glass with his remaining eye. As he continued to drive he looked to this right and realised Aled was frozen in his seat, with blood pouring from the left side of his neck. Even more incredibly, Rob let go of his left eye that was still attached to the optical cord and now hung down on his cheek so that he could steer with his left hand and use his right hand to try and put pressure on the wound to Aled's neck. After about 2 kilometres Rob pulled the convoy over. All-round defence was established, and medical evacuation requested.

Rob and Aled were taken to BIAP for treatment and subsequently flown back through Germany and on to the UK. Rob lost the sight of his left eye. Aled had a piece of shrapnel the size of a ten-pence piece lodged in his neck that stopped about 2 millimetres from his spinal cord. After many hours of delicate surgery it was removed, and he made a full recovery.

Should a bravery award ever be instated for civilians, Rob would be my first nomination.

FOOD, GLORIOUS FOOD

One evening I was in my office when the front door to our villa rang. I answered it, and there was Gloria and a man.

'Hi, stranger, how you doing?' she asked.

Gloria was a contact we had made earlier. She was an American married to a Qatari and ran a food supply company based in Qatar. One of her contracts was supplying food to the US Military in Iraq. The logistics of this was handled by the Sultan Group in Kuwait, and the contract ran into the billions of dollars. She had been in talks with Mishare, who she also knew about bidding for the contract when it was up for renewal shortly. Mishare had omitted to tell Steve or me about this. Gloria had been sent by Mishare to discuss the security element and had brought this guy with her.

He was US Military and was the logistics advisor to General Sanchez, who was the current coalition military commander in Iraq. In the British Military we have a position called the controller, and he is the most senior noncommissioned post. Once he explained this, I understood his role and importance. He went on to explain that the military had been providing the escorts but were considering using private security and he was doing the rounds to establish a shortlist of companies who would be invited to present their plan. He wanted to know our setup and procedures. I showed him around the villa and, most importantly, the ops room, where all was coordinated from. After a few hours of discussing our SOPs (standard operating procedures), he appeared impressed. As part of my brief, I mentioned that at 0400 hrs the next day a team would be deploying out. He expressed a wish to go with it as far as the border to watch the procedure. I stated it was an excellent idea and suggested we all go for a meal and come back later and await the deployment.

As he and Gloria made their way out the front of the villa I quickly ran to the ops room and informed Dave Hill about our intended observers and to warn off the team leader. I then joined Gloria and guest, and we went for a meal.

After a leisurely meal we returned to the villa and killed a few hours chatting about general politics and the Iraq situation. At the appointed time we went to the rear of the villa, where the guys had already loaded weapons to the wagons out of sight.

Sandy Lyle was the team leader. He had been the shooter in the rear of my wagon during the Hit ambush and had shoved James into the footwell. He had become a TL and had proven himself an extremely effective one. He was an ex-lance corporal, and although not exactly the most progressive of careers within the military, he was excellent in the environment we operated. He had led several convoys to a military base called Anaconda northwest of Bagdad within the Sunni Triangle. It was a nasty area. On one of the convoys Sandy had a sixth sense something was not quite right along a stretch of road near a village that had speed bumps in the road. He deployed on foot and walked ahead of the convoy. As he approached a set of speed bumps, he spotted from about 20 metres away a small mound of artillery shells just off the road adjacent to a speed bump. He halted the convoy, and just as he pulled back, the bad guys detonated the IED. Thankfully, Sandy had put enough distance between him and the IED and had prevented what would have certainly been a vehicle caught in the full blast as it slowed to cross the speed bump.

'Good morning,' Sandy said with a broad smile. 'I believe you will be joining us on our trip to the border?'

The team mounted up, and Gloria and the controller followed in their vehicle. I explained that I would not come so that they could get an unbiased look at things without me trying to give them the sales pitch. I felt confident that Sandy would put on a good show and that it portrayed my confidence in the guys. Sandy later reported that all went well and they seemed impressed.

I informed Steve and SO of the potential. I also cautioned that it was a massive project and was no way certain as we were going to be up against the big boys.

Two days later we received an e-mail inviting us to the Marriott Hotel to give a ten-minute presentation on an outline plan. In the e-mail were the basics of the requirement with locations of sixty-four military bases and approximately the number of trailers per month that would supply them.

At the appointed time, about fifty people assembled in a meeting room at the Marriott. There were about fifteen security companies represented. We were briefed that we would have ten minutes to present an outline plan. There would be no questions, and those who impressed the board would be invited back to present a more in-depth plan.

After several companies had been in it was Steve's and my turn. We went in, and there were a couple of chairs in the centre of the room and a long table with about eight people sat behind it. Most were in uniform and a lot of brass. I recognised the controller, and he gave a very brief smile of acknowledgement.

'Gentlemen, you have ten minutes,' stated one of the panel.

'We cannot do this' was the brief and succinct statement from Steve. He paused for effect. 'In fact, we believe there is not a security company in existence that can do this.' This was the tactic we had decided to take.

'Currently the US Military are carrying out this role and committing a huge number of troops in doing so,' I joined in. 'To effectively cover the full requirement we estimate about three thousand personnel would be need. A brigade's strength of men.'

'We propose that SFI will form a consortium along with other security companies. The drills will be laid down by SFI as, modesty aside, we have been leading the way in convoy mitigation and to date have a very successful track record,' Steve continued. 'We will establish back-to-back contracts ensuring standardisation and compliance with other companies and allocate each company their tactical area of responsibility.'

'We believe the military system is tried and tested, and it makes sense to structure the proposed organisation along military lines,' I further explained.

We expanded a little further, but after about four minutes we rose and said 'thank you' and both walked out the room. A cocky approach, but we assessed that if we had tried to go into detail of how we would physically do it, we could not in ten minutes and that what they were looking for was a company with a realistic approach and a higher strategic view. Time would tell if we were to be invited back.

Focus returned to the V94 project and more requests to go and check civil works. The previous week the civil contracts reported that several of their workers had been taken hostage and a ransom of $50,000 had been paid to release them. On the second time this happened, the alleged hostages were found in their homes nearby, and all turned out to be a scam. The civil contractors were changed. All went to show that you really could not trust anyone in Iraq. If there was an angle, someone would exploit it.

SFI were being asked on a regular basis to go and check various parts of the route, and on every occasion, there was a contact. Either a roadside IED or a small-arms attack. Thankfully, no further serious injuries, but we were losing a vehicle at about one a week.

Enough was enough, so I informed our client that SFI would no longer do these fruitless tasks unless there was a definite and clear need to do so. Surprisingly, the client agreed, and for a few weeks no further requests came through.

So 2004 had come to a close, and the V94 had still not moved. We entered 2005, and we still had forty-four guys on standby. We had rotated guys back for leave and gambled that we would not be called forward. All the guys had emergency contact numbers and would return at a drop of a hat.

In early January I received a call to meet the controller at the Marriott. I doubted that he wanted to see us to tell us we were out. Excitement mounted. At the meeting, it was explained that there we two security companies still in the running, SFI and ArmorGroup. The final hurdle was a submission of our operational order for conducting this size of operation. This meant we had to explain on paper exactly how we were going to execute our plan. We had four days to submit.

We returned to the villa to prepare.

'Over to you,' said Steve. 'This is officer-type shit, paperwork and all.'

I had attended JDSC (Junior Division Staff Collage) while in the Army. This was a five-month course where you are taught, amongst many other things, how to put together a plan for a military operation at regimental level. It is called a deliberate estimate. You document all the factors involved and what deductions you draw and hence how you take account of all the factors. You consider such headings as enemy forces (insurgents/criminals), ground (routes, camp locations), time and space, service support (logistics etc.). From your deliberate estimate follows your plan.

I knew we would have one shot at this, so this had to be as comprehensive as possible. The controller had given us some info, which was quite extensive and of course sensitive, as it detailed all the US Military camps and the details of supplies to these camps. The first thing to do was to dissect the info given to identify all the requirements (the mission and implied missions). Unfortunately, it was not a case of handing out segments to a couple of others to go through. To get a full understanding, I thought it best that I did it all so that I had a full view right across everything. If we split it, we were likely to miss something. The truth was that I did not fully rely upon the rest of the guys to fully grasp what was relevant and what was not. Possibly arrogance on my behalf, but the rest of the guys were not former officers, and there is a difference to how these sorts of tasks are approached. Also, modesty aside, I had come in the top 5 per cent of my peers on JDSC, and despite being a more hands-on sort of guy, I was actually quite good at cutting through all the crap and identifying what was really relevant and seeing the big picture, and then being able to sort the detail needed to make it happen.

So I had four days to complete. The first day was spent going through the info provided. Lots of highlighter pens were used in various colours. The next two-and-a-half days were spent working through the factors, deductions, options, and the final plan. Late nights, early mornings, and lots of strong coffee. On day 4 the final document was printed off and bound. It was an A4 size document about two inches thick. A copy was also provided on a disk, as requested.

About an hour before the appointed cutoff the plan was handed in. The simple response we got was, 'We will be in touch.'

Again we were back to waiting.

SOLDIERING ON

Late January 2005 and there were signs the V94 might actually get going. This meant that we would need all forty-four guys ready for this, as well as guys and vehicles to cover the other contracts we had running. In all, we were going to need close on to one hundred men and nearly thirty vehicles. We had been making some good money. We had even paid some dividends to the four partners. I had continued to conduct interviews and had a sizable database of new recruits lined up. Having had experience in Iraq, it was easier to interview, and we were also getting a lot more guys who had private-security experience with other companies. I had started to build a good picture on how some of the companies operated and some of the shortcuts they were taking. Lots of stories of guys not getting paid, some companies self-insuring and then not being able to cover injuries.

We were also getting a lot more enquiries from Japanese companies through JICS. One enquiry from Sumitomo was to provide security to supplies going into Iraq for water treatment plants that were situated all around the outskirts of Baghdad. Unbelievably, this included truckloads of sand. Apparently in Iraq it was the 'wrong' sort of sand that the treatment plants used. This sand came from Dubai. Trust the Japs to sell sand to the Arabs!

We were also approached by an American gentleman who had a couple of trailers that went into Iraq. He had been using a 'rabble' of a security team from Basra who had reported the trailers being hijacked and claiming they had to pay a ransom to get them back. Then they were stating that they were being delayed due to US Military and claiming extra days. What they did not know was he had a tracking system installed and knew they were not where they said they were. They had threatened him if he went with another security company. So he came to SFI.

Sandy Lyle took the first convoy of his trucks, and as expected, just over the border a roadblock of four vehicles and about ten Iraqis met them. We had deployed three vehicles with nine men so were outnumbered. Or at least that is what they must have initially thought. On a predetermined call, four gun trucks appeared off to the right flank, line abreast and dripping with machine guns, all trained on the roadblock.

After a few minutes' standoff, Sandy, cool as a cucumber, got out and walked the front of his vehicle. He raised his arm and casually gestured for the roadblock to disburse and leave. This they did and drove away, tails between their legs. After what was deemed a suitable distance, the gun trucks peeled off the convoy and returned to base. It was a bold move, but we never saw them again, and we completed another ten trips for the client.

Finally the word came, and the team deployed for the V94. I called in Chalky to go over the final plans. As we talked he appeared a little off, and I asked if there was anything wrong. He explained the guys were uneasy as they believed I was a 'cunt' for sending a weak team to Baiji where Rob had lost his hand. After a few seconds of stunned silence, I opened the e-mail I had sent Steve and his reply where he had stated proudly that he alone had made the decision. Thank God I had that e-mail.

'I didn't think you would have done that,' replied Chalky.

'Really?' I asked, looking him in the eye for some sign he really meant that. I respected Chalky, and I would have felt terrible if he and, just as importantly, the guys thought I had made that call.

'Honestly. It didn't sound like the sort of thing you

would be OK with. But Steve has told some of the guys that you made that call.' He appeared to be trying to reassure me. I was gutted that the guys had believed Steve and not doubted that I would have exposed them like that.

'Well, you can tell them that was not the case. OK?' I quietly and calmly said.

'Will do, Boss,' replied Chalky, almost with a renewed vigour in his voice. I did feel somewhat relieved that Chalky appeared to be reassured that his confidence in me had been renewed.

Chalky and his team headed off to link up at the Jordanian border. I was confident that we had a good team and that with the promised US Military assistance in the more dodgy areas we would have a successful mission. It was not without risk, as the level of insurgency seemed to be on the increase, and more worryingly, so was the number of suicide attacks. We had been on standby for nearly five months, and it was now time to conclude this project. An expected three-week journey through some parts of the most dangerous country in the world. Would the overt security presence work and deter any would-be attackers to look for a softer target?

There was a part of me that wanted to be on the job, but with the potential of the US Military contract in the offing and many other enquiries coming in, I needed to be in the villa. Besides, Steve was again AWOL, allegedly more meetings in the UK. Since the start of the year he had hardly been in Kuwait, and when he did come it was not long before he had to return for some reason or other. I was getting pissed off.

There was a part of me that was glad he was not there, as often he would start agreeing to terms that were not sustainable, but on the other hand I needed someone else to help with the workload and decision-making. I was beginning to feel isolated and felt that I was trying to hold up everything on my own. Mishare was never really involved. SO was a serving officer and was due to retire later in the year, and Steve was often AWOL. I had also started to pick up rumours and snip bits of info that some of the guys in the ops room, namely Bertie and Chris, were trying to sort out a contract of their own and splinter off. I had been warned that when there were lucrative contracts, there would be no such thing as loyalty; trust no one. Or was I becoming paranoid?

Following a call from the controller, he came around to the villa one afternoon. Again I could only assume that it was for some good news. I thought about calling Steve but decided to wait until I knew what the situation was.

'Well, SFI is the only one left standing' was the succinct statement from the controller. I stared at him for what seemed like a rude amount of time. I was actually speechless: frozen.

'OK,' I eventually said with a definite gap between the O and the K.

'You're not there yet,' he continued. 'Your op order was sent to the Pentagon for assessment. The response I got was "These guys appear to have their shit wired tight,"' concluded the controller, with a slight whimsical smile on his face.

'"Shit wired tight." I guess that's good, yeah?' I asked.

'They were very impressed and have confidence that SFI would be capable of forming a consortium of security companies to effectively run this,' he replied.

'But we're not there yet, you say?' I said.

'The Pinkerton Act,' he said.

Apparently, some year back there was an incident whereby a private security company, Pinkerton, was guarding US Military assets and they ended up shooting someone. As a result, there was an act passed in the US Senate prohibiting the use of private security for US Military assets.

'It looks like it could be a showstopper, unless we can come up with a way around it,' said the controller. 'We are working on this, but I thought I would let you know where we are up to. Any ideas?' he asked.

'Two ideas immediately spring to mind,' I replied.

I explained that one option was that we would be guarding the civilian drivers and their trucks rather than the cargo that they were carrying. The second was that we would clear a route and if the convoy happened to travel within that cleared area, then all well and good. The controller thought the second option was a bit of a stretch, but the first option was a possibility. He would feed this back in and stated he was quietly confident this was a solution.

I called Steve right after he left and let him know the situation. We both could not believe we were potentially on the verge of a massive contract.

'Then we can sell and kick back on a beach somewhere, drinking daiquiris' was Steve's conclusion.

'One, we are not there yet, and two, we would have to get it up and running before anyone would be remotely interested in buying us out,' I cautioned.

After the phone call to Steve, I sat for some time, contemplating the enormity of what could be. It was potentially a multibillion dollar contract. My mind was racing, thinking of how we would ramp up. How we would need to tie up subcontracts with other companies. We would need a good lawyer. We would need more higher-level planners. Holy shit, this is unbelievable. I did not sleep much that night.

Meanwhile, the V94 convoy was coming to the end of the first week and without incident. It was now about to head into bandit country. Talking to Chalky on the sat phone, I was assured all was going well. The guys were working well together, and the US Military were there in numbers at the choke points. The weather was cold, but the rains had stopped, which was good as it was mostly graded track for about 200 kilometres.

Steve flew back out to Kuwait, and we met up with SO. We discussed recruiting in some more management to help with the potential ramp up. I also raised the matter of potential desertion in the ranks. I explained to Steve and SO that Chris and Bertie were potentially using their position within SFI to line themselves up with a contract of their own and detailed the odd e-mail that had come to light. Steve was reluctant to take it further. I pushed by saying, 'Can we afford not to do anything about it?'

SO agreed that we needed to investigate further. Steve stated he would speak with Bertie, and he believed he would tell him the truth. Naive, I thought.

Later, back in the villa, Steve said, 'You know SO retires later this year?'

'Yeah, August?' I asked.

Steve went on to question what use SO would be after he retired and was no longer the defence attaché. I was again surprised, as Steve and SO went back further than my relationship with Steve.

'So what are you saying? We get rid of SO?' I asked, fully knowing that is what he meant. Kind of ironic that Steve was saying this after SO had already suggested the same about Steve.

'He has been asking me for a pay raise and wants more expenses,' Steve explained. Before I had a chance to comment Steve continued, 'He is like a greedy pig at the trough.' He continued to ramble off a list of grievances against SO.

I was not surprised that Steve wanted to cut the numbers but was surprised at the suddenness of his turn on SO, as there had been no inkling of this brewing.

To maintain my stance that we all started together and that we should all stick together, I offered, 'Look, Steve, SO had his uses in the early days, and we could not have done what we did without him. I think we have all earned our place at the table. Besides, when he retires he can become more actively involved, and if the big one comes off, his experience will be useful.'

Steve said he would speak to Mishare about it and that a possible severance package could be offered.

The following day, SO asked if he could be given the cost of six bottles of whiskey. He had supplied these through his allocation from the embassy, and they were used for payment to some US Military guys at one of the camps to paint our gun trucks black with IR reflective paint. The timing by SO perhaps went to reinforce Steve's feelings. After all, SO was receiving £4,000 a month tax-free for doing not a lot at this stage.

Meanwhile, Steve spoke with Bertie, and as it turns out, Bertie had been in contact talks with another company, but not to set up a contract. He had been offered a job and had decided to accept it. He gave notice to Steve. When Steve told me, he appeared genuinely hurt by the fact that Bertie had jumped ship to another company. No such thing as loyalty, I reminded myself.

'Just when you think you can trust someone,' Steve said as he slumped into the chair, with a despondent look on his face. 'I've known Bertie for over twenty years,' he said.

I felt like saying that I felt on my own as the only ex-officer and with all the other key guys being ex-warrant officers, but as Steve was one of them, I thought better of it and just soldiered on.

To add to the already mounting tension of waiting for news, we were informed that to continue to operate within Iraq we had to register SFI with the Iraqi MOI (Ministry of Interior). As the Iraqis gained more of their sovereignty they began to put in place control measures. This was inevitable and I guess a good thing that there was going to be some form of quality control put in place. But I doubt that better quality would be the end result and that compulsory employment of Iraqi nationals would soon follow. But firstly, the minefield of Iraqi red tape to wade through in order to get SFI registered and legal to operate.

Week 2 of the V94 also passed without incident, and the transit across bandit country went without a hitch. Although Chalky reported that to their front and their rear there had been incidents but sufficiently far enough away as to not impact on progress. So far so good, and another week and it would be complete. Which was a shame, as it was turning out to be an extremely lucrative project.

Previous talk of bringing on an accountant came to fruition, and Huw Davies started. The key point of his CV that caught my eye was under the heading of 'Main Achievements', that he had refrained from placing his hands around his ex-wife's throat during the divorce proceeding. Despite being a qualified accountant, this sort of humour on his CV swung it. I was also glad, as SFI was due to be audited as a registered Kuwaiti company. When Huw took over the accounts, he appeared pleasantly surprised at the health of the bank account. We had just short of one million dollars. I explained that we had wages to cover but also we were due to pay our insurance renewal towards the end of the year, which was about a million, so was building up a reserve to cover.

As well as the Iraqi MOI gaining its feet, it was also becoming more and more difficult to cross the Kuwait/Iraq border with weapons. The Kuwaiti Army was taking more of an interest, and with the changing of regiments at the border, we lost our 'assistance'. On a few occasions they would search vehicles and find weapons, so all weapons were put into one vehicle and we would say it was going to our base in Iraq. The guys would wait until about 4:00 pm, when the guards had their meal, and then try again. The guards were more interested in eating and would wave them through from their guard box. We had a good run, but it was now time to properly consider setting up a base within Iraq.

My to-do list was growing. I was putting plans in place in case we needed to ramp up for the big one. I was going through Iraqi MOI registration, planning on a new base in Iraq, and running the day-to-day operations of SFI. Steve, on the other hand, was again back in UK, allegedly at meetings.

Week 3 of the V94 passed, and as the turbine rolled into the power station in Kirkuk and another, a successful mission was completed. SFI and ALE, along with some help from the US Military, had moved a three hundred ton turbine from Jordan to Kirkuk. Some achievement.

MOI registration was finally completed, and as expected, we were now obliged to employ local Iraqi to make up 10 per cent of the guard force. We had to supply details of the contracts we were running and our staff levels as part of registration. Naturally, we had been a little economical with these details, but nonetheless we were now expected to show at least ten locals on our books. Here, the relationship I had built with my friendly police colonel in Basra paid off. I asked him for ten passport copies of local nationals, which he readily supplied for a fee of $5,000 per month. I do not know who these locals were, but we never saw them and did not want to. They appeared on our trip records and satisfied the MOI requirements.

We were still waiting for news from the controller, but nothing had come through by late March. I turned my attention to a base in Iraq. I arranged a meeting with Jalal, a contact I had made in Basra. We met about 5 kilometres inside Iraq, just off route Tamper. I had explained what I wanted, and he had lined up three locations to view. The first was a fairway into Basra itself and was surrounded by a residential area. Not good at all, so we quickly dismissed and moved on. The second was a walled compound out in the open. Jalal explained that it was one of the properties owned by one of the former Bath party members who we would know as Chemical Ali. It was an excellent location and facilities, but too high profile for my liking, so we again moved on. The final location was a piece of open desert right off route Tamper and about 3 kilometres from the border crossing point. It was an ideal location. The owner was prepared to build a wall around an area 100 metres by 100 metres and wanted $5,000 rent per month. What I liked was that there was open desert between the rear of the location and the border crossing point and only about 1.5 kilometres as the crow flies. In the event of an emergency and possibly being overrun, a fighting withdrawal to the border was a realistic option. Other companies had set up in various locations and had been overrun either by insurgents or angry locals. This location I liked, and it was relatively cheap.

The V94 team returned to the villa, and most returned to the UK for some R&R. The main point was what we were going to do with so many once they had a week or two off and would be asking for the next job. There were several contracts running and a few more bubbling away and nearing signing. We really could do with some news on the big one.

BETRAYAL IS RIFE

One morning Murtaza came to my office and showed me a text message he had received from Chris. It asked Murtaza to price up for six vehicles, eighteen sets of body armour and helmets, and medical trauma kits. I had been working on the water treatment contract, and Chris had been helping. For this project we would need the equipment mentioned in Chris's text. Chris was back in the UK at this time, and I was due to fly back in a few days. I spoke with Steve and showed him the text. We agreed that I would call Chris to a meeting when I went back and confront him.

I flew back two days later and called Chris to meet up the following day. The morning of the meet I received a call from Steve to say he had also flown back and wanted to be at the meeting. He explained that as Chris was brought in by him, he wanted to be there. I had no problem with that stance but could not help but see it as yet another reason for Steve to fly back to the UK.

Chris was already waiting in the foyer of the hotel where we arranged to meet when Steve and I walked in. On seeing both of us, his faced reddened. He sat upright and said, 'I guess I'm getting my marching orders then.'

'Why do you ask that?' asked Steve.

'For both of you to be here, what else can it be?' replied Chris.

'Is there any reason you should be sacked, Chris?' I asked.

'Oh, that sounded very leading, Detective,' stated Chris as he relaxed back in the chair. He paused for a second or two and then said, 'I guess the cat is out of the bag. Murtaza told you?'

'Yep,' said Steve.

Chris explained that he had planned to set up a contract with Dean Sankey, one of our clients, and run it themselves. He appeared very matter of fact about it and showed no remorse.

'Obviously, you are dismissed with immediate effect,' said Steve.

There was very little else said, and Steve and I walked out. As we drove away, Steve was again visibly upset by the events.

'We need to stick together and see this through, Steve,' I tried to reassure. The rest of the trip was silent.

I returned to Kuwait a week later and over the next few weeks did several trips to Jordan. We were still discussing a contract to take fire engines that were being donated to the Iraqi people by the people of Japan. The meetings were held at the Japanese embassy in Amman. After four such meetings we signed and prepared to take a total of twenty-one engines in. They would be taken three at a time on the back of low-bed trailers. It was a short-notice start, and we quickly dispatched a team.

The route was along the main highway from the Jordanian border to a compound on the southwest side of Baghdad. Mostly open desert, but there had been a rise in insurgent activity in the Anbar Province, which formed the first half of the route. The first trip went off without incident. The second trip had travelled no further than about 60 kilometres when a roadside IED detonated. The main blast caught the rear security vehicle. All three guys in the vehicle received shrapnel wounds, but none were life threatening. The driver, John, had most of his triceps of his right arm peeled up his arm, exposing his brachial artery, but fortunately this did not sever. The blast also caught the rear fire engine, and this ironically caught fire. The guys reported a black 5 series BMW that appeared to have been dicking them leading up to the attack. The remaining five trips went without incident.

In mid-April I flew my wife and two kids out to Kuwait, as it was the school Easter holidays. Steve had suggested that I charged their flights to the company account as I had been away for most of the year and that he felt I had earned it. I was not going to turn this down and had booked their economy seats through the company account we had with British Airways. They were to stay in the villa. Steve also unexpectedly flew out and also brought his wife and daughter. My wife explained that she had not seen them on the flight. I knew Steve would have been in business class and assumed he had also flown his wife and daughter business. I half suspected he would have put this through the company account as well. I asked Huw for the BA invoices to sign off. Looking through, I could see the flights for my family. Then I saw Steve's family's flights. The flight code had an F in front of it and appeared very expensive. I immediately knew what it meant. Just as that point, Steve walked into the office, having dropped his family off at the SAS Radisson hotel.

'Steve, any idea what this F means?' I asked, fully expecting him to openly admit the flights and in a way the opportunity for him to come clean.

Without blinking, he replied, 'No idea, they flew business class, which I paid for.' He then walked out and left the villa. I was stunned at the bare-faced cheek that he simply expected me to accept it when the invoice in front of me told me that they had all just flown first class and booked to the company. I thought I would give him the benefit of the doubt and check that he had booked it through the company to get the company discount with the intention of paying it back. I checked with Huw, and he knew nothing about it. I then checked with Sandy, who booked the flights. She showed me the e-mail chain when Steve had requested Sandy to book the flights and in bold red type when Steve has specified first-class seats for all three.

I called Steve. 'You really know how to take the piss, don't you?' I said.

'What?' he replied with as much shock as he could muster.

'Please, just have the balls to tell me when I show you the invoice. But to lie to my face. What a twat,' I replied and hung up.

For the next week I never saw Steve. His family flew back to the UK, as did mine. He returned to the villa, and when he walked into the office, he was sheepish and disappeared into his room. Eventually he came out.

'We need to speak about an Iraq base,' he stated.

'Yes, we do,' I replied. 'That land near the border appears to be the best option. I have written down some points but suggest we get Shep and John in and we can go through what we need.'

Later that evening we sat and discussed what we would need, from portacabin offices, sleeping accommodation, water and electrical supply to a full escape plan. It was agreed that over the next few days we would put together some costs and come up with a budget to set up. We each had our tasks.

I flew to the UAE for a few days for a meeting with a potential client. On my return, I was informed that Sandy had been sacked. I called her to find out what had happened. She informed me that Steve had accused her of cocking up the flight booking. I was livid. I asked where Steve was, only to be informed he had flown back to the UK for a meeting.

A couple of days later I received a call from the controller. It was not good news. As the current situation stands, private security would not be allowed to protect US Military food convoys. The controller could hear the disappointment in my voice. He tried to console me with compliments on our application and professionalism. It was little comfort. I was gutted.

After a day or so of self-pity I did what I have done several times in my life. Picked myself up, dusted off, and set off again. I decided that if I gave up now, the company would fall apart. I felt a responsibility to ensure we carried on. Business as usual. There was a core team that had been there since the start, and I for one could not let them down. I knew Shep needed the work for personal reasons. Chalky had been solid throughout and deserved the company to succeed and provide him employment for as long as he wanted it.

I called a meeting with Shep and Dave to discuss the plans for setting the Iraq base. I asked Shep how he had got on with costs for sleeping accommodation. He informed me that we did not need them as we would be moving into one of the UK Military bases near Umm Qasr Port.

'What?' I asked.

'Steve has arranged that we will move into a compound there,' Shep explained.

I was stunned. 'When did all this happen?' I asked.

'Steve called this morning and said it was all arranged,' replied Shep. He could tell I was totally unaware and pissed off, again.

It transpired that Steve had contacted an old Royal Artillery mate of his whose unit was based in a small compound near Umm Qasr Port. It was a good location, but we had discussed moving in with military, as this was only ever going to be a short-term measure as each unit did short rotations and the next one may not be so obliging.

I arranged to go up and meet with Steve's contact. I took a small team with me to look, including Shep, and he also knew this contact. When we got there the compound was just big enough to accommodate the unit that was stationed there. We were allocated a small piece of ground just big enough to place a few containers.

When I returned to the villa I tried to contact Steve. He was not answering his phone and did not respond to e-mails or text messages. The next few weeks there was very little contact, and when I was able to get hold of him we would agree one course of action, only to find that he was then heading off in another direction. The guys in the villa were clearly unsettled by this, and the atmosphere became unpleasant.

One day Huw came into my office and said, 'You two have to get this sorted. You need to communicate.'

I opened up my laptop and showed Huw several e-mails I had written to Steve, trying to discuss various matters, without any response.

'OK, sorry, I thought you were both not speaking,' he replied.

'Huw, I am trying to get things sorted, but Steve just keeps blanking me or agreeing one thing and then doing another,' I said.

I could now see that the business relationship was deteriorating. It was not that long ago that Steve was talking about sidelining SO. Was he still intending to do this? I doubted it as Steve always needs someone to ally with. I concluded that I was now public enemy number 1. I had curtailed his expense blagging too many times. I suspected that Steve and SO were now scheming and that I would be the target. SO had shown his colours on many an occasion, and it was evident he went whichever way he could gain the most from. I had seen SO want to turn against Steve early on and had seen Steve wanting to oust SO. I was now a fly in the ointment. I was the one stopping both Steve and SO from milking the company and from pulling the wool over Mishare's eyes. Perhaps I was naive and should have jumped on the bandwagon. But I was sure had I allowed the floodgates to open, there would not be much of a company to milk, and besides after all is said and done, it was not right. I do not profess to be a saint, but Mishare had placed a lot of trust in us, and although he had been repaid well, I still believed he deserved our trust. But still I did not believe that Steve would betray me. I came into this venture with my eyes wide open, and the milking of the expenses and all the trips back to the UK, although annoying, were not totally unexpected. So with all we had discussed about trust and friendship, I concluded that Steve would not stab me in the back.

We had earned some good money, but I had now passed the point where the money meant more than my sanity. The past few months had been extremely stressful. I was trying to secure the big one and at the same time run the company. Steve had managed to give the impression he was involved but in reality had little or no involvement and, as far as business development went, had produced nothing in the way of solid leads from all the 'meetings' he had been attending in the UK. Regardless of what Steve's intentions were, I was getting close to the point where I was wanting to get out. If we could secure one or more of the potential contracts with the Japs, it would see us through to the end of the year, and that would probably be the time to exit, stage right.

In August I returned to the UK for a couple of weeks' break. Steve was supposed to be out in Kuwait, but it came as no surprise when I received a call from him and he asked for me to meet him. He said that SO would be at the meeting and suggested we met at a mutual friend's office. So a meeting with both of them on neutral ground and not at Steve's house. There is a saying that states, 'If it looks like an ambush, then it is.' I assessed that their approach was to sideline me. They could not simply kick me out. I had too much info they needed, not to mention I had kept under my control the database of potential recruits. If this was going to be the night of the long knives, then I needed an exit strategy that got me the best result. Firstly, I had to second-guess what their tack would be. The database was one ace card I held. They needed me to continue on this, and until they build up their own database of recruits, they needed 'my guys'. I was also the only one who fully understood the insurance side and the claims that were under process for the injured guys. I would suggest that we needed a permanent representation in the UK. The fact that Steve was in the UK that often meant that he could have done this, but it would mean he would have to actually do something and get involved with casualties and the aftermath, which he shied away from. They would suggest that I fill this role. This was my best guess of their tactics. I wanted to see out the year, but if there was going to be a fight for control, I may come out on top but would have very little support. SO would back Steve, as he knew how to work Steve to his best advantage. Steve would offer SO higher salary in return for support. There would be no thought as to whether this was best business practice. Steve could see no further than blagging his next expenses claim, let alone planning future business expenditure.

After some long deliberation, I decided I had had enough. I wanted out. If Steve was going to stab me in the back, I could no longer trust him in anything. My biggest fear all along was fatalities. We had been lucky. We had some serious injuries, and I felt bad enough about that. I was scared that Steve would do something like the run to Baiji, where he sent an under-strength crew and Rob had lost his hand. Plus, it was going to get harder to operate within Iraq. No doubt the MOI would increase the percentage of locals, and I did not want to be part of that.

At the appointed time, we met. The atmosphere was tense. Steve could not look me in the eye and just stared down at the table. SO, on the other hand, was far more aggressive in his body language. He was sat up and slightly forward and staring straight at me, eyes wide. I leant forward to meet his gaze, then laughed and said, 'So what is all this about?'

SO appeared to visibly stutter and sat back slightly. 'Look, the relationship between you and Steve has broken down to the point that it is damaging the company.'

Steve continued to look down at the table. I had a flashback to the time we had a head-to-head with Ian in the early days. Then, Steve said very little, as if not to appear to be the main orchestrator. Again he was saying nothing.

'Is this your opinion as well, Steve?' I asked.

Steve had both his hands palm down on the table. He raised his left hand slightly and rotated his hand in the direction of SO as if for SO to continue, which he obligingly did. 'We have spoken about this before, and there is a need for someone senior to be based in UK to look after this end,' said SO.

'Steve, would you be interested in this role?' I asked with a smile on my face. SO frowned as in disbelief that I had not grasped what all this was about. I had second-guessed their tack and knew exactly what they were angling towards. I just wanted Steve to look me in the eye and tell me himself.

'Steve, you have anything to say?' I asked, leaning forward, lowering my head, and looking up towards Steve to catch his gaze. There was a slight pause, and then he shrugged his shoulders slightly, like a petulant child who had just been caught out doing something he shouldn't have.

I took a second to weigh up the situation. It was obvious which way this was going, and I could play with them for a while and make them squirm, but there was little point.

'So, Steve, you've decided to do the one thing you promised you would never do,' I said. Steve looked at me with a theatrical puzzled look on his face as if to make out he didn't know what I meant. 'Trust,' I said, looking him straight in the eye. He immediately looked back down at the table.

This was done. There was no more to be said.

'OK, so I will do the UK bit. I will handle the insurance and recruitment and any other business needing attention in the UK,' I said in a matter-of-fact way. 'Obviously, I will take a reduced salary as I will no longer be going into Iraq. I suggest five thousand per month and expenses for travel etc.' I did not want them dictating terms, so I stated my terms first.

'Agreed,' Steve said, finally breaking his silence.

'And dividends when paid out to partners, and that's for as long as SFI is in existence,' I concluded.

'Agreed,' Steve said. With that, he stood up and said he had to take a call, pulling his phone out of his pocket.

I turned to SO and said, 'I want your assurance as an officer and a gentleman that you will honour what has just been agreed here.' I said this as I extended my hand to shake on it.

'You have my word,' said SO as he took my hand and shook. My blood instantly boiled as I just knew that what he really meant to say was, 'You will be cut out as soon as I can manipulate Steve into it.' It was not so much the fact that he was going to double-cross me for financial gain; it was the fact that I had challenged him to be honourable as a holder of the Queen's commission, and he had discredited the very nature of it.

I returned home and told my wife of the meeting. I stated that at best the agreement would last for one year and then be broken. I assessed that this is what Steve would have agreed with SO to ease his conscience.

Over the next couple of months I continued to deal with the insurance claims and recruit. Every so often, I would get an e-mail from the ops room, asking to send a few more guys off the database. Each month my salary would not be paid and I had to ask what the hold-up was, and eventually, after two or three requests it would be paid.

As 2005 drew to a close, I started to look at the insurance renewal. I requested the number of staff employed so that I could base our quote on. This information was not forthcoming. Steve would not answer any of my e-mails, and when I contacted the ops room, I was simply told to contact Steve. This was the start of the 'phase me out' plan. I then discovered that Steve had set Huw, the accountant, on renewing the insurance. One less matter I had control of. I also had no doubt that Steve had tasked someone to start building a database of recruits. But the ops room kept asking for fresh guys every now and again, so perhaps they were not.

In January 2006 I contacted the ops room as I was anxious that the insurance cover had been put in place. A short while later I received an e-mail from SO stating that as I was no longer a board member, I had no right in asking such details. I responded that I did not know I had been voted off the board. Not that we really ever had a board to be voted off. He replied that Steve, Mishare, and SO had a meeting and had voted me off the board and that Steve was supposed to have informed me. Of course Steve had failed to inform me. I expressed my concern that I was not informed or invited to this meeting, which fell on deaf ears.

I could see that Steve and SO were going to squeeze me out as soon as they could. I could see that they would milk the situation as much as they could and Mishare would be blind to what they would be doing. I liked Mishare and did not want to see him being taken for a ride. I needed to see him face to face. Not only to warn him of the potential dangers of Steve and SO being let loose with a blank cheque book, but I also I wanted to hear it from him what really happened at the meeting where I was voted out. I booked a flight to Kuwait and booked into a hotel. I did not book through SFI as I did not want Steve knowing I was going, and besides, the booking would have been blocked, I had no doubt.

In late January I flew to Kuwait. After booking into the hotel I took a taxi to the Chamber of Commerce, where Mishare's office was located. After some initial pleasantries I turned the conversation to the meeting where I was supposedly voted off the board. Mishare explained that Steve had approached him stating that I wanted to return home to the UK to spend more time with my family. But then had changed it to the fact that we were arguing all the time over what direction we wanted to take the company. They had then convened a meeting, where Mishare stated he would go with the majority vote. So had I actually have been there, the outcome would have been the same.

'Mishare, you are a lawyer by trade, and you know that I am a former detective. What I have here is a file of evidence. You can take it or leave it, but I think you ought to know what potentially you are exposed to once I am out of the picture,' I said, handing him a folder I had prepared. I had trawled my e-mails and various documents that showed the attitude and actions of Steve and SO. I went through each one with Mishare to try and get him to understand that without any cheques and balances Steve would effectively rape the company of any spare cash, run up debt, and commercially cripple the company.

I covered how Steve had tried to take £40,000 for each of us, saying we had put this into the company at the start. I had stopped him, as we had not. I showed some e-mails on how Steve wanted to run some projects off book so as not to declare dividends and hide cash from Mishare. I had not allowed that to happen. There were twenty main examples I had documented and given. There were numerous others of a lesser nature I had not.

I did this for two reasons. Firstly, because I genuinely did not want Mishare to be dragged into a whole pile of crap, as he was a local Kuwaiti and would be left to pick up the pieces. But secondly, there was a part of me that wanted Mishare to get cross and drag Steve and SO in and force the situation, whereby I came out on top and they would be the ones sent running with their tails between their legs. However, there was the other part of me that did not want to be left with it all to manage and just wanted out. I guess this way I could always have a clear conscience that I had tried to warn Mishare and had at least put up a bit of a fight.

Mishare appeared interested in what I had to say and wrote down lots of notes. He stated he would look into some of the points as he already had some concerns. However, it was clear that he did not want to get involved between the disagreements of Steve and me. I could only assume that to date he had been paid his initial investment back and had received some dividends, and so he was happy that things would continue in that vein.

I returned to my hotel and reflected that it was actually all over. Mishare was not going to do anything, and it was only a matter of time before I received notice that my involvement in SFI was deemed over as ordained by Steve. Strangely enough, I was OK with that. I had a good run and had enjoyed the past two-and-a-half years. I had a few close scrapes, and all in all perhaps it was the right time to get out, while I was still intact.

Over the next several months the requests for guys continued to come in from the ops room, which really surprised me. I would have thought by now they would have formed their own database. It had been nearly ten months since our meeting, and although every month I had to chase for my salary, it did come. However, the one-year point was looming, and sure enough the signs came. I was asked if I could e-mail the full database list of all those I had interviewed. Naturally, I declined but knew this was a precursor to a notice that my salary would cease at the one-year point following the meeting. True to form, I received an e-mail from SO declaring such, and exactly a year after the meeting my SFI e-mail account was deactivated, and my last salary was received. In the twelve months since the meeting, no further dividends were received, not that I expected any.

AFTERMATH

A year later I joined ALE as the operations manager. James had called me one day and offered me the job. So the next chapter in my life began, and I moved out to Abu Dhabi. I had been there for about six months when one evening, I received a call from a Kuwaiti number. I was surprised to hear Mishare's voice.

After some pleasantries he asked, 'Do you know where Steve is?'

'No,' I replied. 'Why?'

'He owes me some money' came his not so surprising news.

He went on to explain that Steve had led Mishare to believe there were some big contracts about to be signed and that the company needed some investment. Mishare had put some of his own personal money in, as well as money from one of his companies, Moya Projects, which was the official fourth partner of SFI. There were also large debts run up with Nissan, who supplied the security vehicles, and with a travel agent Steve had set up a contract with. As Moya Projects and Mishare were the local contact, the creditors came after Mishare.

'I'm afraid to ask, but how much money are you down?' I asked as I cringed in anticipation of several hundred thousand dollars.

'I am personally owed half a million, and Moya Projects is owed four-and-half million,' Mishare replied.

'Four-and-half million dollars, US.' I wanted clarifying.

'Yes, a total of five million dollars, US,' confirmed Mishare.

I was staggered. I did not think even Steve could do

that in only just under two years. That was going some. I was even more staggered that Mishare had allowed it to go that far, least not as I had warned him. But still, five million!

I explained that the last time I had spoken to Steve was at the meeting when I was stabbed in the back. I did not know where he was or what he was up to.

'I have an arrest warrant for him if he ever comes to Kuwait,' Mishare stated. 'If you hear anything about him, please let me know.'

'Sure, will do,' I replied.

I did not hear from Mishare again.

As I reflected on the situation, I could not help feeling a certain amount of satisfaction that during the two-and-a-half years I was involved and pretty much running the show, we had turned a profit of just under two million dollars. In the two years after I was sidelined, Steve had taken SFI to five million in debt. I had entered the whole affair not knowing much about business and thinking it to be a dark art, but on reflection, it was not that difficult as long as you maintained a sensible and prudent approach. We had taken some risks and cut some corners because if we had not, SFI would never have seen the light of day, especially in Iraq, with no systems in place. We ploughed our own furrow and made it happen.

Modesty aside, I had done bloody well. Steve had opened some doors, and with the belief that he was going to develop contracts, I forged ahead on the operational setup. When we got the first contract and then got the go-ahead, I flew in a team, equipped them from scratch, and deployed within four days. On our first convoy, I defused a roadside bomb that helped cement our reputation. But more importantly for me, I realised that I could operate in the business world. I negotiated contracts, ran budgets of millions of dollars, and kept the SFI on a sound business footing.

Was it just the case that after I left the whole Iraq situation changed that it was no longer viable to run the sort of company like SFI? Was it just bad luck that conspired that lead to SFI getting into such debt? I have my opinion, but I will leave that for others to decide.

But the one overriding lesson I learnt: trust no one!

Printed by Amazon Italia Logistica S.r.l.
Torrazza Piemonte (TO), Italy